N_o
N_{ature}

No
Nature

New and Selected Poems

GARY SNYDER

Pantheon Books
New York & San Francisco

Grateful acknowledgment is made to the following
for permission to reprint previously published material:

New Directions Publishing Corporation: Poems from *The Back Country,* Copyright © 1957,
1958, 1959, 1960, 1961, 1962, 1963, 1964, 1965, 1966, 1967 by Gary Snyder; *Regarding Wave,*
Copyright © 1967, 1968, 1969, 1970 by Gary Snyder; *Myths & Texts,* Copyright © 1960,
1978 by Gary Snyder; and *Turtle Island,* Copyright © 1969, 1971, 1972, 1973, 1974 by Gary
Snyder are used by permission of New Directions Publishing Corporation, 80 Eighth
Avenue, New York, New York 10011, to whom any permission requests for these specific
poems should be addressed.

North Point Press: Selections from *Axe Handles,* Copyright © 1983 by Gary Snyder; from
Left Out in the Rain: New Poems 1947–1985, Copyright © 1986 by Gary Snyder; and from
Riprap and *Cold Mountain Poems,* Copyright © 1958, 1959, 1965 by Gary Snyder were
published by North Point Press and are reprinted here by arrangement with Farrar, Straus
& Giroux, Inc.

Library of Congress Cataloging in Publication Data

Snyder, Gary.
No nature : new and selected poems / Gary Snyder.
Includes index.
I. Title.
PS3569.N88N6 1992
811'.54—dc20
ISBN 0-679-74252-2

Book design by
Fearn Cutler & M. Kristen Bearse

Manufactured in the United States of America

PREFACE

What's intimate? The feet and hands, one's confection of thoughts, knowledges, and memories; the kitchen and the bedding. And there is one's language. How wonderful to be born to become a Native Speaker, to be truly native of something. I've been at home with the same language—eased by it, amused by it, surfing on it, no matter where I lived, through the years.

These poems belong to the west coast tongue, Anglo-franco American Indo-European, and to the emergent Pacific culture. Some of them owe much to my readings of Chinese and Japanese short poems, some are instructed by ethnopoetics, and most are in the debt of the mid-twentieth-century masters. I also make my bows to Native American song, story, and subsistence; to the persistence of the old growth forests of the far west; to the snowy peaks of the Pacific crest, and to some great teachers.

No Nature. Human societies each have their own nutty fads, mass delusions, and enabling mythologies. Daily life still gets done. Wild nature is probably equally goofy, with a stunning variety of creatures somehow getting by in all these landscapes. Nature also means the physical universe, including the urban, industrial, and toxic. But we do not easily *know* nature, or even know ourselves. Whatever it actually is, it will not fulfil our conceptions or assumptions. It will dodge our expectations and theoretical models. There is no single or set "nature" either as "the natural world" or "the nature of things." The greatest respect we can pay to nature is not to trap it, but to acknowledge that it eludes us and that our own nature is also fluid, open, and conditional.

Hakuin Zenji puts it "self-nature that is no nature/ . . . far beyond mere doctrine." An open space to move in, with the whole body, the whole mind. My gesture has been with language.

March 6, 1992

CONTENTS

Kāli

Back

from Left Out in the Rain

No Nature

from

Riprap

&

Cold
Mountain
Poems

Riprap

riprap: a cobble of stone laid on steep
slick rock to make a trail for horses in
the mountains

MID-AUGUST AT SOURDOUGH
MOUNTAIN LOOKOUT

Down valley a smoke haze
Three days heat, after five days rain
Pitch glows on the fir-cones
Across rocks and meadows
Swarms of new flies.

I cannot remember things I once read
A few friends, but they are in cities.
Drinking cold snow-water from a tin cup
Looking down for miles
Through high still air.

THE LATE SNOW & LUMBER STRIKE
OF THE SUMMER OF FIFTY-FOUR

Whole towns shut down
        hitching the Coast road, only gypos
Running their beat trucks, no logs on
Gave me rides. Loggers all gone fishing
Chainsaws in a pool of cold oil
On back porches of ten thousand
Split-shake houses, quiet in summer rain.
Hitched north all of Washington
Crossing and re-crossing the passes
Blown like dust, no place to work.

Climbing the steep ridge below Shuksan
        clumps of pine
        float out the fog
No place to think or work
        drifting.

On Mt. Baker, alone
In a gully of blazing snow:
Cities down the long valleys west
Thinking of work, but here,
Burning in sun-glare
Below a wet cliff, above a frozen lake,
The whole Northwest on strike
Black burners cold,
The green-chain still,
I must turn and go back:
        caught on a snowpeak
        between heaven and earth
And stand in lines in Seattle.
Looking for work.

PIUTE CREEK

One granite ridge
A tree, would be enough
Or even a rock, a small creek,
A bark shred in a pool.
Hill beyond hill, folded and twisted
Tough trees crammed
In thin stone fractures
A huge moon on it all, is too much.
The mind wanders. A million
Summers, night air still and the rocks
Warm.   Sky over endless mountains.
All the junk that goes with being human
Drops away, hard rock wavers
Even the heavy present seems to fail
This bubble of a heart.
Words and books
Like a small creek off a high ledge
Gone in the dry air.

A clear, attentive mind
Has no meaning but that
Which sees is truly seen.
No one loves rock, yet we are here.
Night chills. A flick
In the moonlight
Slips into Juniper shadow:
Back there unseen
Cold proud eyes
Of Cougar or Coyote
Watch me rise and go.

MILTON BY FIRELIGHT

Piute Creek, August 1955

"O hell, what do mine eyes
      with grief behold?"
Working with an old
Singlejack miner, who can sense
The vein and cleavage
In the very guts of rock, can
Blast granite, build
Switchbacks that last for years
Under the beat of snow, thaw, mule-hooves.
What use, Milton, a silly story
Of our lost general parents,
      eaters of fruit?

The Indian, the chainsaw boy,
And a string of six mules
Came riding down to camp
Hungry for tomatoes and green apples.
Sleeping in saddle-blankets
Under a bright night-sky
Han River slantwise by morning.
Jays squall
Coffee boils

In ten thousand years the Sierras
Will be dry and dead, home of the scorpion.
Ice-scratched slabs and bent trees.
No paradise, no fall,
Only the weathering land
The wheeling sky,
Man, with his Satan
Scouring the chaos of the mind.
Oh Hell!

Fire down
Too dark to read, miles from a road
The bell-mare clangs in the meadow
That packed dirt for a fill-in
Scrambling through loose rocks
On an old trail
All of a summer's day.

ABOVE PATE VALLEY

We finished clearing the last
Section of trail by noon,
High on the ridge-side
Two thousand feet above the creek
Reached the pass, went on
Beyond the white pine groves,
Granite shoulders, to a small
Green meadow watered by the snow,
Edged with Aspen—sun
Straight high and blazing
But the air was cool.
Ate a cold fried trout in the
Trembling shadows. I spied
A glitter, and found a flake
Black volcanic glass—obsidian—
By a flower. Hands and knees
Pushing the Bear grass, thousands
Of arrowhead leavings over a
Hundred yards. Not one good
Head, just razor flakes
On a hill snowed all but summer,
A land of fat summer deer,
They came to camp. On their
Own trails. I followed my own
Trail here. Picked up the cold-drill,
Pick, singlejack, and sack
Of dynamite.
Ten thousand years.

WATER

Pressure of sun on the rockslide
Whirled me in dizzy hop-and-step descent,
Pool of pebbles buzzed in a Juniper shadow,
Tiny tongue of a this-year rattlesnake flicked,
I leaped, laughing for little boulder-color coil—
Pounded by heat raced down the slabs to the creek
Deep tumbling under arching walls and stuck
Whole head and shoulders in the water:
Stretched full on cobble—ears roaring
Eyes open aching from the cold and faced a trout.

HAY FOR THE HORSES

He had driven half the night
From far down San Joaquin
Through Mariposa, up the
Dangerous mountain roads,
And pulled in at eight a.m.
With his big truckload of hay
          behind the barn.
With winch and ropes and hooks
We stacked the bales up clean
To splintery redwood rafters
High in the dark, flecks of alfalfa
Whirling through shingle-cracks of light,
Itch of haydust in the
          sweaty shirt and shoes.
At lunchtime under Black oak
Out in the hot corral,
—The old mare nosing lunchpails,
Grasshoppers crackling in the weeds—
"I'm sixty-eight" he said,
"I first bucked hay when I was seventeen.
I thought, that day I started,
I sure would hate to do this all my life.
And dammit, that's just what
I've gone and done."

THIN ICE

Walking in February
A warm day after a long freeze
On an old logging road
Below Sumas Mountain
Cut a walking stick of alder,
Looked down through clouds
On wet fields of the Nooksack—
And stepped on the ice
Of a frozen pool across the road.
It creaked
The white air under
Sprang away, long cracks
Shot out in the black,
My cleated mountain boots
Slipped on the hard slick
—like thin ice—the sudden
Feel of an old phrase made real—
Instant of frozen leaf,
Icewater, and staff in hand.
"Like walking on thin ice—"
I yelled back to a friend,
It broke and I dropped
Eight inches in

NOOKSACK VALLEY

February 1956

At the far end of a trip north
In a berry-pickers cabin
At the edge of a wide muddy field
Stretching to the woods and cloudy mountains,
Feeding the stove all afternoon with cedar,
Watching the dark sky darken, a heron flap by,
A huge setter pup nap on the dusty cot.
High rotten stumps in the second-growth woods
Flat scattered farms in the bends of the Nooksack
River. Steelhead run now
                    a week and I go back
Down 99, through towns, to San Francisco
                              and Japan.
All America south and east,
Twenty-five years in it brought to a trip-stop
Mind-point, where I turn
Caught more on this land—rock tree and man,
Awake, than ever before, yet ready to leave.
              damned memories,
Whole wasted theories, failures and worse success,
Schools, girls, deals, try to get in
To make this poem a froth, a pity,
A dead fiddle for lost good jobs.
              the cedar walls
Smell of our farm-house, half built in '35.
Clouds sink down the hills
Coffee is hot again. The dog
Turns and turns about, stops and sleeps.

ALL THROUGH THE RAINS

That mare stood in the field—
A big pine tree and a shed,
But she stayed in the open
Ass to the wind, splash wet.
I tried to catch her April
For a bareback ride,
She kicked and bolted
Later grazing fresh shoots
In the shade of the down
Eucalyptus on the hill.

MIGRATION OF BIRDS

April 1956

It started just now with a hummingbird
Hovering over the porch two yards away
                        then gone,
It stopped me studying.
I saw the redwood post
Leaning in clod ground
Tangled in a bush of yellow flowers
Higher than my head, through which we push
Every time we come inside—
The shadow network of the sunshine
Through its vines. White-crowned sparrows
Make tremendous singings in the trees
The rooster down the valley crows and crows.
Jack Kerouac outside, behind my back
Reads the *Diamond Sutra* in the sun.
Yesterday I read *Migration of Birds*;
The Golden Plover and the Arctic Tern.
Today that big abstraction's at our door
For juncoes and the robins all have left,
Broody scrabblers pick up bits of string
And in this hazy day
Of April summer heat
Across the hill the seabirds
Chase Spring north along the coast:
Nesting in Alaska
In six weeks.

TŌJI

Shingon temple, Kyoto

Men asleep in their underwear
Newspapers under their heads
Under the eaves of Tōji,
Kobo Daishi solid iron and ten feet tall
Strides through, a pigeon on his hat.

Peering through chickenwire grates
At dusty gold-leaf statues
A cynical curving round-belly
Cool Bodhisattva—maybe Avalokita—
Bisexual and tried it all, weight on
One leg, haloed in snake-hood gold
Shines through the shadow
An ancient hip smile
Tingling of India and Tibet.

Loose-breasted young mother
With her kids in the shade here
Of old Temple tree,
Nobody bothers you in Tōji;
The streetcar clanks by outside.

KYOTO: MARCH

A few light flakes of snow
Fall in the feeble sun;
Birds sing in the cold,
A warbler by the wall. The plum
Buds tight and chill soon bloom.
The moon begins first
Fourth, a faint slice west
At nightfall. Jupiter half-way
High at the end of night-
Meditation. The dove cry
Twangs like a bow.
At dawn Mt. Hiei dusted white
On top; in the clear air
Folds of all the gullied green
Hills around the town are sharp,
Breath stings. Beneath the roofs
Of frosty houses
Lovers part, from tangle warm
Of gentle bodies under quilt
And crack the icy water to the face
And wake and feed the children
And grandchildren that they love.

THE SAPPA CREEK

Old rusty-belly thing will soon be gone
Scrap and busted while we're still on earth—
But here you cry for care,
We paint your steel shelves red
& store the big brass valves with green
Wheel handles. Dustpan and wastecan
Nestle in the corner—
Contemplating what to throw away.
Rags in bales, the final home for bathrobes,
Little boy bluejeans and housewife dresses
Gay print splash—all wiping oil off floorplates,
Dangling from hip pockets like a scalp.
Chipping paint, packing valves, going nuts,
Eating frozen meat, we wander greasy nurses
Tending sick and nervous old & cranky ship.

GOOFING AGAIN

Goofing again
I shifted weight the wrong way
flipping the plank end-over
dumping me down in the bilge
& splatting a gallon can
of thick sticky dark red
italian deck paint
over the fresh white bulkhead.
such a trifling move
& such spectacular results.
now I have to paint the wall again
& salvage only from it all a poem.

CARTAGENA

Rain and thunder beat down and flooded the streets
We danced with Indian girls in a bar,
        water half-way to our knees,
The youngest one slipped down her dress and danced
        bare to the waist,
The big negro deckhand made out with his girl on his lap
        in a chair her dress over her eyes
Coca-cola and rum, and rainwater all over the floor.
In the glittering light I got drunk and reeled through
        the rooms,
And cried, "Cartagena! swamp of unholy loves!"
And wept for the Indian whores who were younger than me,
        and I was eighteen,
And splashed after the crew down the streets wearing
        sandals bought at a stall
And got back to the ship, dawn came,
        we were far out at sea.

Colombia 1948—Arabia 1958

Lay down these words
Before your mind like rocks.
          placed solid, by hands
In choice of place, set
Before the body of the mind
          in space and time:
Solidity of bark, leaf, or wall
          riprap of things:
Cobble of milky way,
          straying planets,
These poems, people,
          lost ponies with
Dragging saddles
          and rocky sure-foot trails.
The worlds like an endless
          four-dimensional
Game of *Go*.
          ants and pebbles
In the thin loam, each rock a word
          a creek-washed stone
Granite: ingrained
          with torment of fire and weight
Crystal and sediment linked hot
          all change, in thoughts,
As well as things.

Cold
Mountain Poems

Kanzan, or Han-shan, "Cold Mountain" takes his name from where he lived. He is a mountain madman in an old Chinese line of ragged hermits. When he talks about Cold Mountain he means himself, his home, his state of mind. He lived in the T'ang dynasty—traditionally A.D. 627–650, although Hu Shih dates him 700–780. This makes him roughly contemporary with Tu Fu, Li Po, Wang Wei, and Po Chü-i. His poems, of which three hundred survive, are written in T'ang colloquial: rough and fresh. The ideas are Taoist, Buddhist, Zen. He and his sidekick Shih-te (Jittoku in Japanese) became great favorites with Zen painters of later days—the scroll, the broom, the wild hair and laughter. They became Immortals and you sometimes run onto them today in the skidrows, orchards, hobo jungles, and logging camps of America.

The path to Han-shan's place is laughable,
A path, but no sign of cart or horse.
Converging gorges—hard to trace their twists
Jumbled cliffs—unbelievably rugged.
A thousand grasses bend with dew,
A hill of pines hums in the wind.
And now I've lost the shortcut home,
Body asking shadow, how do you keep up?

(1)

In a tangle of cliffs I chose a place—
Bird-paths, but no trails for men.
What's beyond the yard?
White clouds clinging to vague rocks.
Now I've lived here—how many years—
Again and again, spring and winter pass.
Go tell families with silverware and cars
"What's the use of all that noise and money?"

(2)

In the mountains it's cold.
Always been cold, not just this year.
Jagged scarps forever snowed in
Woods in the dark ravines spitting mist.
Grass is still sprouting at the end of June,
Leaves begin to fall in early August.
And here am I, high on mountains,
Peering and peering, but I can't even see the sky.

(3)

Men ask the way to Cold Mountain
Cold Mountain: there's no through trail.
In summer, ice doesn't melt
The rising sun blurs in swirling fog.
How did I make it?
My heart's not the same as yours.
If your heart was like mine
You'd get it and be right here.

(6)

I settled at Cold Mountain long ago,
Already it seems like years and years.
Freely drifting, I prowl the woods and streams
And linger watching things themselves.
Men don't get this far into the mountains,
White clouds gather and billow.
Thin grass does for a mattress,
The blue sky makes a good quilt.
Happy with a stone underhead
Let heaven and earth go about their changes.

(7)

Clambering up the Cold Mountain path,
The Cold Mountain trail goes on and on:
The long gorge choked with scree and boulders,
The wide creek, the mist-blurred grass.
The moss is slippery, though there's been no rain
The pine sings, but there's no wind.

Who can leap the world's ties
And sit with me among the white clouds?

(8)

❧

I have lived at Cold Mountain
These thirty long years.
Yesterday I called on friends and family:
More than half had gone to the Yellow Springs.
Slowly consumed, like fire down a candle;
Forever flowing, like a passing river.
Now, morning, I face my lone shadow:
Suddenly my eyes are bleared with tears.

(10)

❧

Spring-water in the green creek is clear
Moonlight on Cold Mountain is white
Silent knowledge—the spirit is enlightened of itself
Contemplate the void: this world exceeds stillness.

(11)

❧

In my first thirty years of life
I roamed hundreds and thousands of miles.
Walked by rivers through deep green grass
Entered cities of boiling red dust.
Tried drugs, but couldn't make Immortal;

25

Read books and wrote poems on history.
Today I'm back at Cold Mountain:
I'll sleep by the creek and purify my ears.

(12)

❧

I can't stand these bird-songs
Now I'll go rest in my straw shack.
The cherry flowers out scarlet
The willow shoots up feathery.
Morning sun drives over blue peaks
Bright clouds wash green ponds.
Who knows that I'm out of the dusty world
Climbing the southern slope of Cold Mountain?

(13)

❧

There's a naked bug at Cold Mountain
With a white body and a black head.
His hand holds two book-scrolls,
One the Way and one its Power.
His shack's got no pots or oven,
He goes for a walk with his shirt and pants askew.
But he always carries the sword of wisdom:
He means to cut down senseless craving.

(15)

❧

Cold Mountain is a house
Without beams or walls.

The six doors left and right are open
The hall is blue sky.
The rooms all vacant and vague
The east wall beats on the west wall
At the center nothing.

Borrowers don't bother me
In the cold I build a little fire
When I'm hungry I boil up some greens.
I've got no use for the kulak
With his big barn and pasture—
He just sets up a prison for himself.
Once in he can't get out.
Think it over—
You know it might happen to you.

(16)

Once at Cold Mountain, troubles cease—
No more tangled, hung-up mind.
I idly scribble poems on the rock cliff,
Taking whatever comes, like a drifting boat.

(19)

Some critic tried to put me down—
"Your poems lack the Basic Truth of Tao"
And I recall the old-timers
Who were poor and didn't care.
I have to laugh at him,
He misses the point entirely,

Men like that
Ought to stick to making money.

(20)

❧

I've lived at Cold Mountain—how many autumns.
Alone, I hum a song—utterly without regret.
Hungry, I eat one grain of Immortal-medicine
Mind solid and sharp; leaning on a stone.

(21)

❧

My home was at Cold Mountain from the start,
Rambling among the hills, far from trouble.

Gone, and a million things leave no trace
Loosed, and it flows through the galaxies
A fountain of light, into the very mind—
Not a thing, and yet it appears before me:
Now I know the pearl of the Buddha-nature
Know its use: a boundless perfect sphere.

(23)

❧

When men see Han-shan
They all say he's crazy
And not much to look at
Dressed in rags and hides.

They don't get what I say
& I don't talk their language.
All I can say to those I meet:
"Try and make it to Cold Mountain."

(24)

For Lloyd Reynolds and David French

from

Myths

&

Texts

So that not only this our craft
is in danger to be set at nought;
but also the temple of the great
Goddess Diana should be despised,
and her magnificence should be destroyed,
whom all Asia and the world worshippeth.

—Acts 19:27

Logging

The morning star is not a star
Two seedling fir, one died
                    Io, Io,
Girdled in wistaria
Wound with ivy
                    "The May Queen
Is the survival of
A pre-human
Rutting season"

The year spins
Pleiades sing to their rest
                    at San Francisco
                    dream
                    dream
Green comes out of the ground
Birds squabble
Young girls run mad with the pine bough,
                    Io

> But ye shall destroy their altars,
> break their images, and cut down their groves.
> —*Exodus 34:13*

The ancient forests of China logged
   and the hills slipped into the Yellow Sea.
Squared beams, log dogs,
   on a tamped-earth sill.
San Francisco 2 x 4s
   were the woods around Seattle:
Someone killed and someone built, a house,
   a forest, wrecked or raised
All America hung on a hook
   & burned by men, in their own praise.

Snow on fresh stumps and brush-piles.
The generator starts and rumbles
               in the frosty dawn
I wake from bitter dreams,
Rise and build a fire,
Pull on and lace the stiff cold boots
Eat huge flapjacks by a gloomy Swede
In splintery cookhouse light
          grab my tin pisspot hat
Ride off to the show in a crummy-truck
And start the Cat.

"Pines grasp the clouds with iron claws
like dragons rising from sleep"
250,000 board-feet a day
If both Cats keep working
& nobody gets hurt

❧

"Lodgepole Pine: the wonderful reproductive
power of this species on areas over which its
stand has been killed by fire is dependent upon
the ability of the closed cones to endure a fire
which kills the tree without injuring its seed.
After fire, the cones open and shed their seeds
on the bared ground and a new growth springs up."

Stood straight
            holding the choker high
As the Cat swung back the arch
            piss-firs falling,
Limbs snapping on the tin hat
            bright D caught on
Swinging butt-hooks
            ringing against cold steel.

Hsü Fang lived on leeks and pumpkins.
Goosefoot,
        wild herbs,
                fields lying fallow!

But it's hard to farm
Between the stumps:
The cows get thin, the milk tastes funny,
The kids grow up and go to college
They don't come back.
            the little fir-trees do

            Rocks the same blue as sky
Only icefields, a mile up,
                are the mountain
Hovering over ten thousand acres
Of young fir.

Pines, under pines,
>   Seami Motokiyo
>   The Doer stamps his foot.
>   A thousand board-feet
Bucked, skidded, loaded—
(Takasago, Ise) float in a mill pond;
A thousand years dancing
Flies in the saw kerf.

Cliff by Tomales Bay
Seal's slick head
>   head shoulders breasts
>   glowing in night saltwater
Skitter of fish, and above, behind the pines,
Bear grunts, stalking the Pole-star.

Foot-whack on polished boards
Slide and stop; drum-thump.
"Today's wind moves in the pines"
>   falling
And skidding the red-bark pine.
Clouds over Olallie Butte
Scatter rain on the Schoolie flat.
A small bear slips out the wet brush
>   crosses the creek
Seami, Kwanami,
>   Gone too.
Through the pines.

❧

Felix Baran
Hugo Gerlot
Gustav Johnson
John Looney
Abraham Rabinowitz
Shot down on the steamer Verona
For the shingle-weavers of Everett
      the Everett Massacre November 5 1916

Ed McCullough, a logger for thirty-five years
Reduced by the advent of chainsaws
To chopping off knots at the landing:
"I don't have to take this kind of shit,
Another twenty years
      and I'll tell 'em to shove it"
      (he was sixty-five then)
In 1934 they lived in shanties
At Hooverville, Sullivan's Gulch.
When the Portland-bound train came through
The trainmen tossed off coal.

"Thousands of boys shot and beat up
For wanting a good bed, good pay,
      decent food, in the woods—"
No one knew what it meant:
"Soldiers of Discontent."

Ray Wells, a big Nisqually, and I
      each set a choker
On the butt-logs of two big Larch
In a thornapple thicket and a swamp.
      waiting for the Cat to come back,
"Yesterday we gelded some ponies
"My father-in-law cut the skin on the balls
"He's a Wasco and don't speak English
"He grabs a handful of tubes and somehow
      cuts the right ones.
"The ball jumps out, the horse screams
"But he's all tied up.
The Caterpillar clanked back down.
In the shadow of that racket
      diesel and iron tread
I thought of Ray Wells' tipi out on the sage flat
The gelded ponies
Healing and grazing in the dead white heat.

Each dawn is clear
Cold air bites the throat.
Thick frost on the pine bough
Leaps from the tree
        snapped by the diesel

Drifts and glitters in the
        horizontal sun.
In the frozen grass
        smoking boulders
        ground by steel tracks.
In the frozen grass
        wild horses stand
        beyond a row of pines.
The D8 tears through piss-fir,
Scrapes the seed-pine
                chipmunks flee,
A black ant carries an egg
Aimlessly from the battered ground.
Yellowjackets swarm and circle
Above the crushed dead log, their home.
Pitch oozes from barked
        trees still standing,
Mashed bushes make strange smells.
Lodgepole pines are brittle.
Camprobbers flutter to watch.

A few stumps, drying piles of brush;
Under the thin duff, a toe-scrape down
Black lava of a late flow.
Leaves stripped from thornapple
Taurus by nightfall.

A green limb hangs in the crotch
Of a silver snag,
Above the Cats,
         the skidders and thudding brush,
Hundreds of butterflies
Flit through the pines.
"You shall live in square
         gray houses in a barren land
         and beside those square gray
         houses you shall starve."
—Drinkswater. Who saw a vision
At the high and lonely center of the earth:
Where Crazy Horse
         went to watch the Morning Star,
& the four-legged people, the creeping people,
The standing people and the flying people
Know how to talk.
I ought to have eaten
Whale tongue with them.
         they keep saying I used to be a human being
"He-at-whose-voice-the-Ravens-sit-on-the-sea."
Sea-foam washing the limpets and barnacles
Rattling the gravel beach
Salmon up creek, bear on the bank,
Wild ducks over the mountains weaving
In a long south flight, the land of
Sea and fir tree with the pine-dry
Sage-flat country to the east.
Han Shan could have lived here,
         & no scissorbill stooge of the
         Emperor would have come trying to steal
         his last poor shred of sense.
On the wooded coast, eating oysters
Looking off toward China and Japan
"If you're gonna work these woods
Don't want nothing
That can't be left out in the rain—"

The groves are down
                    cut down
Groves of Ahab, of Cybele
Pine trees, knobbed twigs
        thick cone and seed
        Cybele's tree this, sacred in groves
Pine of Seami, cedar of Haida
Cut down by the prophets of Israel
        the fairies of Athens
        the thugs of Rome
                    both ancient and modern;
Cut down to make room for the suburbs
Bulldozed by Luther and Weyerhaeuser
Crosscut and chainsaw
        squareheads and finns
        high-lead and cat-skidding
Trees down
Creeks choked, trout killed, roads.

Sawmill temples of Jehovah.
Squat black burners 100 feet high
Sending the smoke of our burnt
Live sap and leaf
To his eager nose.

❧

Lodgepole
        cone/seed waits for fire
And then thin forests of silver-gray.
        in the void
        a pine cone falls
Pursued by squirrels
What mad pursuit! What struggle to escape!

Her body a seedpod
Open to the wind
"A seed pod void of seed
We had no meeting together"
        so you and I must wait
Until the next blaze
Of the world, the universe,
Millions of worlds, burning
        —oh let it lie.

Shiva at the end of the kalpa:
Rock-fat, hill-flesh, gone in a whiff.
Men who hire men to cut groves
Kill snakes, build cities, pave fields,
Believe in god, but can't
Believe their own senses
Let alone Gautama. Let them lie.

Pine sleeps, cedar splits straight
Flowers crack the pavement.
        Bada Shanren
(A painter who watched Ming fall)
        lived in a tree:
"The brush
May paint the mountains and streams
Though the territory is lost."

Hunting

first shaman song

In the village of the dead,
Kicked loose bones
        ate pitch of a drift log
        (whale fat)
Nettles and cottonwood. Grass smokes
            in the sun
Logs turn in the river
        sand scorches the feet.

Two days without food, trucks roll past
        in dust and light, rivers
        are rising.
Thaw in the high meadows. Move west in July.

Soft oysters rot now, between tides
        the flats stink.

I sit without thoughts by the log-road
Hatching a new myth
watching the waterdogs
        the last truck gone.

this poem is for birds

Birds in a whirl, drift to the rooftops
Kite dip, swing to the seabank fogroll
Form: dots in air changing line from line,
              the future defined.
Brush back smoke from the eyes,
              dust from the mind,
With the wing-feather fan of an eagle.
A hawk drifts into the far sky.
A marmot whistles across huge rocks.
Rain on the California hills.
Mussels clamp to sea-boulders
Sucking the Spring tides

Rain soaks the tan stubble
Fields full of ducks

Rain sweeps the Eucalyptus
Strange pines on the coast
              needles two to the bunch
The whole sky whips in the wind
Vaux Swifts
Flying before the storm
Arcing close hear sharp wing-whistle
Sickle-bird
              pale gray
              sheets of rain slowly shifting
              down from the clouds,
Black Swifts.
              —the swifts cry
As they shoot by, See or go blind!

"As for me I am a child of the god of the mountains."

A bear down under the cliff.
She is eating huckleberries.
They are ripe now
Soon it will snow, and she
Or maybe he, will crawl into a hole
And sleep. You can see
Huckleberries in bearshit if you
Look, this time of year
If I sneak up on the bear
It will grunt and run

The others had all gone down
From the blackberry brambles, but one girl
Spilled her basket, and was picking up her
Berries in the dark.
A tall man stood in the shadow, took her arm,
Led her to his home. He was a bear.
In a house under the mountain
She gave birth to slick dark children
With sharp teeth, and lived in the hollow
Mountain many years.
             snare a bear: call him out:
honey-eater
forest apple
light-foot
Old man in the fur coat, Bear! come out!
Die of your own choice!
Grandfather black-food!
                 this girl married a bear
Who rules in the mountains, Bear!
                 you have eaten many berries
                 you have caught many fish
                 you have frightened many people

Twelve species north of Mexico
Sucking their paws in the long winter
Tearing the high-strung caches down
Whining, crying, jacking off
(Odysseus was a bear)

Bear-cubs gnawing the soft tits
Teeth gritted, eyes screwed tight
                    but she let them.
Til her brothers found the place
Chased her husband up the gorge
Cornered him in the rocks.
Song of the snared bear:
        "Give me my belt.
        "I am near death.
        "I came from the mountain caves
        "At the headwaters,
        "The small streams there
        "Are all dried up.

—I think I'll go hunt bears.
                "hunt bears?
Why shit Snyder,
You couldn't hit a bear in the ass
            with a handful of rice!"

this poem is for deer

"I dance on all the mountains
On five mountains, I have a dancing place
When they shoot at me I run
To my five mountains"

Missed a last shot
At the Buck, in twilight
So we came back sliding
On dry needles through cold pines.
Scared out a cottontail
Whipped up the winchester
Shot off its head.
The white body rolls and twitches
In the dark ravine
As we run down the hill to the car.
                         deer foot down scree
Picasso's fawn, Issa's fawn,
Deer on the autumn mountain
Howling like a wise man
Stiff springy jumps down the snowfields
Head held back, forefeet out,
Balls tight in a tough hair sack
Keeping the human soul from care
                on the autumn mountain
Standing in late sun, ear-flick
Tail-flick, gold mist of flies
Whirling from nostril to eyes.

Home by night
                drunken eye
Still picks out Taurus
Low, and growing high:
            four-point buck
Dancing in the headlights

on the lonely road
A mile past the mill-pond,
With the car stopped, shot
That wild silly blinded creature down.

Pull out the hot guts
                with hard bare hands
While night-frost chills the tongue
                and eye
The cold horn-bones.
The hunter's belt
                just below the sky
Warm blood in the car trunk.
Deer-smell,
                the limp tongue.

Deer don't want to die for me.
                I'll drink sea-water
Sleep on beach pebbles in the rain
Until the deer come down to die
                in pity for my pain.

Sealion, salmon, offshore—
Salt-fuck desire driving flap fins
North, south, five thousand miles
Coast, and up creek, big seeds
Groping for inland womb.

Geese, ducks, swallows,
                          paths in the air
I am a frozen addled egg on the tundra

My petrel, snow-tongued
          kiss her a brook her mouth
of smooth pebbles her tongue a bed
          icewater flowing in that
Cavern dark, tongue drifts in the creek
                          —blind fish

On the rainy boulders
On the bloody sandbar
I ate the spawned-out salmon
I went crazy
Covered with ashes
Gnawing the girls breasts
Marrying women to whales
Or dogs, I'm a priest too
I raped your wife
I'll eat your corpse

Flung from demonic wombs
           off to some new birth
A million shapes—just look in any
           biology book.
And the hells below mind
           where ghosts roam, the heavens
Above brain, where gods & angels play
           an age or two
& they'll trade with you,
Who wants heaven?
           rest homes like that
Scattered all through the galaxy.

       "I kill everything
        I fear nothing but wolves
        From the mouth of the Cowlitz
                   to its source,
        Only the wolves scare me,
        I have a chief's tail"
—Skunk.
        "We carry deer-fawns in our mouths
         We carry deer-fawns in our mouths
         We have our faces blackened"
—Wolf-song.
"If I were a baby seal
                every time I came up
I'd head toward shore—"

Now I'll also tell what food
we lived on then:

Mescal, yucca fruit, pinyon, acorns,
prickly pear, sumac berry, cactus,
spurge, dropseed, lip fern, corn,
mountain plants, wild potatoes, mesquite,
stems of yucca, tree-yucca flowers, chokecherries,
pitahaya cactus, honey of the ground-bee,
honey, honey of the bumblebee,
mulberries, angle-pod, salt, berries,
berries of the one-seeded juniper,
berries of the alligator-bark juniper,
wild cattle, mule deer, antelopes,
white-tailed deer, wild turkeys, doves, quail,
squirrels, robins, slate-colored juncoes,
song sparrows, wood rats, prairie dogs,
rabbits, peccaries, burros, mules, horses,
buffaloes, mountain sheep, and turtles.

How rare to be born a human being!
Wash him off with cedar-bark and milkweed
        send the damned doctors home.
Baby, baby, noble baby
Noble-hearted baby

One hand up, one hand down
"I alone am the honored one"
Birth of the Buddha.
And the whole world-system trembled.
"If that baby really said that,
I'd cut him up and throw him to the dogs!"
said Chao-chou the Zen Master. But
Chipmunks, gray squirrels, and
Golden-mantled ground squirrels
        brought him each a nut.
Truth being the sweetest of flavors.

Girls would have in their arms
A wild gazelle or wild wolf-cubs
And give them their white milk,
        those who had new-born infants home
Breasts still full.
Wearing a spotted fawnskin
        sleeping under trees
        bacchantes, drunk
On wine or truth, what you will,
Meaning: compassion.
Agents: man and beast, beasts
Got the buddha-nature
All but
Coyote.

Burning

second shaman song

Squat in swamp shadows.
       mosquitoes sting;
         high light in cedar above.
Crouched in a dry vain frame
    —thirst for cold snow
    —green slime of bone marrow
Seawater fills each eye

Quivering in nerve and muscle
Hung in the pelvic cradle
Bones propped against roots
A blind flicker of nerve

Still hand moves out alone
Flowering and leafing
        turning to quartz
Streaked rock   congestion of karma
The long body of the swamp.
A mud-streaked thigh.

Dying carp biting air
      in the damp grass,
River recedes. No matter.

Limp fish sleep in the weeds
The sun dries me as I dance

Maudgalyâyana saw hell

Under the shuddering eyelid
Dreams gnawing the nerve-strings,
The mind grabs and the shut eye sees:
Down dimensions floating below sunlight,
Worlds of the dead, Bardo, mind-worlds
& horror of sunless cave-ritual
Meeting conscious monk bums
Blown on winds of karma from hell
To endless changing hell,
Life and death whipped
On this froth of reality (wind & rain
Realms human and full of desire) over the cold
Hanging enormous unknown, below
Art and History and all mankind living thoughts,
Occult & witchcraft evils each all true.
The thin edge of nature rising fragile
And helpless with its love and sentient stone
And flesh, above dark drug-death dreams.

Clouds I cannot lose, we cannot leave.
We learn to love, horror accepted.
Beyond, within, all normal beauties
Of the science-conscious sex and love-receiving
Day-to-day got vision of this sick
Sparkling person at the inturned dreaming
Blooming human mind
Dropping it all, and opening the eyes.

✿

Maitreya the future Buddha

He's out stuck in a bird's craw
                last night
Wildcat vomited his pattern on the snow.

Who refused to learn to dance, refused
To kiss you long ago. You fed him berries
But fled, the red stain on his teeth;
And when he cried, finding the world a Wheel—
            you only stole his rice,
Being so small and gray. He will not go,
But wait through fish scale, shale dust, bone
         of hawk and marmot,
            caught leaves in ice,
Til flung on a new net of atoms:
Snagged in flight
Leave you hang and quiver like a gong

Your empty happy body
Swarming in the light

Face in the crook of her neck
              felt throb of vein
Smooth skin, her cool breasts
All naked in the dawn
                    "byrdes
sing forth from every bough"
              where are they now
And dreamt I saw the Duke of Chou

The Mother whose body is the Universe
Whose breasts are Sun and Moon,
              the statue of Prajna
From Java: the quiet smile,
The naked breasts.

"Will you still love me when my
      breasts get big?"
the little girl said—

"Earthly Mothers and those who suck
the breasts of earthly mothers are mortal—
but deathless are those who have fed
at the breast of the Mother of the Universe."

※

John Muir on Mt. Ritter:

After scanning its face again and again,
I began to scale it, picking my holds
With intense caution. About half-way
To the top, I was suddenly brought to
A dead stop, with arms outspread
Clinging close to the face of the rock
Unable to move hand or foot
Either up or down. My doom
Appeared fixed. I MUST fall.
There would be a moment of
Bewilderment, and then,
A lifeless rumble down the cliff
To the glacier below.
My mind seemed to fill with a
Stifling smoke. This terrible eclipse
Lasted only a moment, when life blazed
Forth again with preternatural clearness.
I seemed suddenly to become possessed
Of a new sense. My trembling muscles
Became firm again, every rift and flaw in
The rock was seen as through a microscope,
My limbs moved with a positiveness and precision
With which I seemed to have
Nothing at all to do.

"If, after obtaining Buddhahood, anyone in my land
   gets tossed in jail on a vagrancy rap, may I
   not attain highest perfect enlightenment.

   wild geese in the orchard
   frost on the new grass

"If, after obtaining Buddhahood, anyone in my land
   loses a finger coupling boxcars, may I
   not attain highest perfect enlightenment.

   mare's eye flutters
   jerked by the lead-rope
   stone-bright shoes flick back
   ankles trembling: down steep rock

"If, after obtaining Buddhahood, anyone in my land
   can't get a ride hitch-hiking all directions, may I
   not attain highest perfect enlightenment.

   wet rocks buzzing
   rain and thunder southwest
   hair, beard, tingle
   wind whips bare legs
   we should go back
   we don't

Spikes of new smell driven up nostrils
Expanding & deepening, ear-muscles
Straining and grasping the sounds
Mouth filled with bright fluid coldness
Tongue crushed by the weight of its flavors
        —the Nootka sold out for lemon drops
(What's this talk about not understanding!
        you're just a person who refuses to see.)

Poetry a riprap on the slick rock of metaphysics
"Put a Spanish halter on that whore of a mare
& I'll lead the bitch up any trail"

(how gentle! He should have whipped her first)

        the wind turns.
        a cold rain blows over the shale
        we sleep in the belly of a cloud.
(you think sex art and travel are enough?
                you're a skinful of cowdung)

South of the Yellow River the Emperor Wu
Set the army horses free in the mountain pastures,
Set the Buffalo free on the Plain of the Peach Grove.
Chariots and armor were smeared with blood
        and put away. They locked up
        the Arrows bag.
Smell of crushed spruce and burned snag-wood.
        remains of men,
Bone-chopped foul remains, thick stew
Food for crows—
        (blind, deaf, and dumb!
        shall we give him another chance?)

At Nyahaim-kuvara
Night has gone
Traveling to my land
        —that's a Mohave night

Our night too, you think brotherhood
Humanity & good intentions will stop it?
As long as you hesitate, no place to go.

Bluejay, out at the world's end
        perched, looked, & dashed
Through the crashing: his head is squashed.
        symplegades, the *mumonkwan,*
It's all vagina dentata
        (Jump!)
"Leap through an Eagle's snapping beak"

Actaeon saw Dhyana in the Spring.

        it was nothing special,
    misty rain on Mt. Baker,
        Neah Bay at low tide.

Stone-flake and salmon.
The pure, sweet, straight-splitting
                    with a ping
Red cedar of the thick coast valleys
Shake-blanks on the mashed ferns
                    the charred logs
Fireweed and bees
An old burn, by new alder
Creek on smooth stones,
Back there a Tarheel logger farm.
(High country fir still hunched in snow)

From Siwash strawberry-pickers in the Skagit
Down to the boys at Sac,
Living by the river
            riding flatcars to Fresno,
Across the whole country
Steep towns, flat towns, even New York,
And oceans and Europe & libraries & galleries
And the factories they make rubbers in
This whole spinning show
            (among others)
Watched by the Mt. Sumeru L.O.

From the middle of the universe
& them with no radio.
"What is imperfect is best"
            silver scum on the trout's belly
            rubs off on your hand.
It's all falling or burning—
            rattle of boulders
            steady dribbling of rocks down cliffs
            bark chips in creeks
Porcupine chawed here—
                    Smoke
From Tillamook a thousand miles
Soot and hot ashes. Forest fires.
Upper Skagit burned I think 1919

Smoke covered all northern Washington.
  lightning strikes, flares,
Blossoms a fire on the hill.
Smoke like clouds. Blotting the sun
Stinging the eyes.
The hot seeds steam underground
  still alive.

"Wash me on home, mama"
                    —song of the Kelp.
A chief's wife
Sat with her back to the sun
On the sandy beach, shredding cedar-bark.
Her fingers were slender
She didn't eat much.

"Get foggy
We're going out to dig
Buttercup roots"

Dream, Dream,
Earth! those beings living on your surface
none of them disappearing, will all be transformed.
When I have spoken to them
when they have spoken to me, from that moment on,
their words and their bodies which they
usually use to move about with, will all change.
I will not have heard them. Signed,
                    (   )
                    Coyote

Sourdough mountain called a fire in:
Up Thunder Creek, high on a ridge.
Hiked eighteen hours, finally found
A snag and a hundred feet around on fire:
All afternoon and into night
Digging the fire line
Falling the burning snag
It fanned sparks down like shooting stars
Over the dry woods, starting spot-fires
Flaring in wind up Skagit valley
From the Sound.
Toward morning it rained.
We slept in mud and ashes,
Woke at dawn, the fire was out,
The sky was clear, we saw
The last glimmer of the morning star.

the myth

Fire up Thunder Creek and the mountain—
                    Troy's burning!
The cloud mutters
The mountains are your mind.
The woods bristle there,
Dogs barking and children shrieking
Rise from below.
Rain falls for centuries
Soaking the loose rocks in space
Sweet rain, the fire's out
The black snag glistens in the rain
& the last wisp of smoke floats up
Into the absolute cold
Into the spiral whorls of fire
The storms of the Milky Way
"Buddha incense in an empty world"

Black pit cold and light-year
Flame tongue of the dragon
Licks the sun

The sun is but a morning star

Crater Mt. L.O. 1952–Marin-an 1956

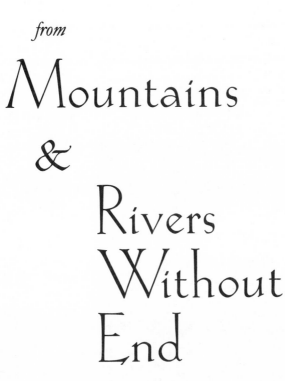

from

Mountains

&

Rivers
Without
End

BUBBS CREEK HAIRCUT

High ceilingd and the double mirrors, the
      calendar a splendid alpine scene—scab barber—
in staind white barber gown, alone, sat down, old man
A summer fog gray San Francisco day
I walked right in. On Howard street
                  haircut a dollar twenty-five.
Just clip it close as it will go.
      "now why you want your hair cut back like that."
      —well I'm going to the Sierras for a while
Bubbs Creek and on across to upper Kern.
      he wriggled clippers
"Well I been up there. I built the cabin
      up at Cedar Grove. In nineteen five."
      old haircut smell.

Next door. Goodwill.
      where I came out.
A search for sweater and a stroll
      in the board & concrete room of
      unfixed junk downstair—
All emblems of the past—too close—
      heaped up in chilly dust and bare bulb glare
Of tables, wheelchairs, battered trunks & lamps
& pots that boiled up coffee nineteen ten, *things*
Swimming on their own & finally freed
      from human need. Or?
      waiting a final flicker of desire
To tote them out once more. Some freakish use.
The Master of the limbo drag-legged watches
      making prices
      to the people seldom buy.
The sag-asst rocker has to make it now. Alone.

      A few days later drove with Locke
down San Joaquin, us barefoot in the heat

stopping for beer and melon on the way
                  the Giant Orange,
rubber shreds of cast truck retreads on the pebble
shoulder, highway ninety-nine.
                              Sierras marked by cumulus
                              in the east.
car coughing in the groves,   six thousand feet:
down to Kings River Canyon; camped at Cedar Grove.
               hard granite canyon walls that
               leave no scree.

Once tried a haircut at the Barber College too—
Sat half an hour before they told me
                  white men use the other side.
Goodwill. St.Vincent de Paul.
                  Salvation Army up the coast
For mackinaws and boots and heavy socks
       —Seattle has the best for logger gear
Once found a pair of good tricouni
                  at the under-the-public market store.
                  Mark Tobey's scene,
                        torn down I hear—
And Filson jacket with a birdblood stain.

A.G. and me got winter clothes for almost nothing
           at Lake Union, telling the old gal
           we was on our way
To work the winter out up in B.C.
                  hitch-hiking home the
Green hat got a ride (of that more later)

hiking up Bubbs Creek saw the trail crew tent
in a scraggly grove of creekside lodgepole pine
             talked to the guy, he says
"If you see McCool on the other trailcrew over there
tell him Moorehead says to go to hell."
late snow that summer. Crossing the scarred bare
           shed of Forester Pass

                  the winding rock-braced switchbacks
dive in snowbanks, we climb on where
                        pack trains have to dig or wait,
a half iced-over lake, twelve thousand feet
                  its sterile boulder bank
but filled with leaping trout:
                  reflections wobble in the
mingling circles always spreading out
            the crazy web of wavelets makes sense
            seen from high above.
a deva world of sorts—it's high
                  it is a view that few men see, a point
      bare sunlight
      on the spaces
empty sky
                  moulding to fit the shape of what ice left
of fire-thrust, or of tilted, twisted, faulted
                  cast-out from this lava belly globe.

The boulder in my mind's eye is a chair.
                        . . . why was the man drag legg'd?
King of Hell
      or is it a paradise of sorts, thus freed
From acting out the function some
                  creator / carpenter
Thrust on a thing to think he made, himself,
            an object always "chair" ?
                  Sinister ritual histories.
            is the Mountain God a gimp?
The halting metrics   and the ritual limp.
                  Good   Will?

Daughter of mountains, stoopd.
      moon breast Parvati

            mountain thunder speaks
            hair tingling static as the lightning lashes
            is neither word of love or wisdom;

though this be danger: hence thee fear.
                    Some flowing girl
whose slippery dance
en trances Shiva
                    —the valley spirit | Anahita,
                            Sarasvati,
dark and female gate of all the world
water that cuts back quartzflake sand
                    soft is the dance that melts the
mat-haired mountain sitter
                            to leap in fire
& make of sand a tree
            of tree a board, of board (ideas!)
            somebody's rocking chair.
a room of empty sun of peaks and ridges
a universe of junk, all left alone.

The hat I always take on mountains:
When we came back down through Oregon
                    (three years before)
At nightfall in the Siskiyou few cars pass

A big truck stopped a hundred yards above
        "Siskiyou Stoneware" on the side
The driver said
He recognized my old green hat.
I'd had a ride
                with him two years before
A whole state north
                when hitching down to Portland
                        from Warm Springs.

Allen in the rear on straw
forgot salami   and we went on south
all night—in many cars—to Berkeley in the dawn.

            upper Kern River country now after nine days walk
            it finally rain.

                     we ran on that other trail crew
               setting up new camp in the drizzly pine
               cussing & slapping bugs, 4 days from road,
               we saw McCool, & he said tell that Moorehead

          KISS MY ASS
     we squatted smoking by the fire.
               "I'll never get a green hat now"
     the foreman says   fifty mosquitoes sitting on the brim

                     they must like green.
     & two more days of thundershower and cold
               (on Whitney hair on end
               hail stinging barelegs in the blast of wind
               but yodel off the summit echoes clean)

          all this comes after:

Purity of the mountains and goodwills.
The diamond drill of racing icemelt waters
          and bumming trucks & watching

Buildings raze
          the garbage acres burning at the Bay
          the girl who was the skid-row
Cripple's daughter—

                out of the memory of smoking pine
The lotion and the spittoon glitter rises
Chair turns and in the double mirror waver
The old man cranks me down and cracks a chuckle

               "Your Bubbs Creek haircut, boy."

THE BLUE SKY

"Eastward from here,

beyond Buddha-worlds ten times as
numerous as the sands of the Ganges
there is a world called
    PURE AS LAPIS LAZULI
its Buddha is called Master of Healing,
    AZURE RADIANCE TATHAGATA

It would take you twelve thousand summer vacations
driving a car due east all day every day
to reach the *edge* of the lapis lazuli realm of
Medicine Old Man Buddha
East. Old Man Realm
East across the sea, yellow sand land
Coyote Old Man land
Silver, and stone blue.

Blue.   [blavus, bhel, belo, "bright colors of the flames"
    flauus   flamen / brahman
    Beltane, "blue fire"—]

Sky.
    [Germanic skuma "cloudy / foamy"
    Sanskrit *sku* "covered"
    skewed (pied)   skewbald (. . . "Stewball")
    skybald / piebald]

        Horse with lightning feet, a mane like
        distant rain, the turquoise horse,
        a black star for an eye
        white shell teeth

Pony that feeds on the pollen of flowers
may he
make thee whole.

Heal hale whole (unblemished . . . kailo) *"holy"*

   Namo bhagavate bhaishajyaguru-vaidurya-
      prabharajaya tathagata arhate samyak
      sambuddhaya tadyatha *om bhaishajye*
         bhaishajye bhaishajya samudgate
               svaha

⤳

Shades of blue through the day.

T'u chüeh   a border tribe near China
Türc
Turquoise: a hydrous phosphate of aluminum
             a little copper
             a little iron—

   Whole, Whole, Make Whole!
   blue land flaming stone-
   Man
      eastward—
         sodium, aluminum, calcium, sulfur.

⤳

In the reign of the Emperor Nimmyo
when Ono-no-Komachi the strange girl poet
was seventeen, she set out looking for her father
who had become a buddhist wanderer. She took ill
on her journey, and sick in bed one night saw

AZURE RADIANCE THUS-COME MEDICINE MASTER

in a dream. He told her she would find a hotsprings
on the bank of the Azuma river in the Bandai mountains
that would cure her; and she'd meet her father there.

◡

"Enchantment as strange as
the Blue up above" my rose of San Antone

Tibetans say that goddesses have lapis lazuli hair

Azure   O.F. azur
                 Arabic lazaward
                 Persian lazhward, "lapis lazuli"
—blue bead charms against the evil eye—

    (Tim and Kim and Don and I were talking about
    what an awful authoritarian garb Doctors
    and Nurses wear, really, how spooky it is.
    "What *should* they wear?"

            —"masks and feathers!")

◡

Ramana Maharshi Dream

I was working as a wood cutter by a crossroads—Ko-san
was working with me—we were sawing and splitting the
firewood. An old man came up the lane alongside a mud
wall—he shouted a little scolding at some Zen monks who
were piling slash by the edge of the woods. He came over
and chatted with us, a grizzled face—neither eastern or
western; or both. He had a glass of buttermilk in his
hand. I asked him "Where'd you get that buttermilk?"
I'd been looking all over for buttermilk. He said,
"At the O K Dairy, right where you leave town."

Medicine. mederi, Indo-european me- "to measure"
   "Maya"—Goddess illusion-wisdom fishing net

Celestial. arched cover . . . *kam.*
Heaven. heman . . . *kam.*
(*comrade.* under the same sky / tent / curve. *kam,* a bent
curved bow,
Kama, God of Love   "Son of Maya"
         bow of flowers.

> *sky blue*
> *right in the rocks too—*
> *lazuli bunting*
> *sea-blue*
> *hazy-hills blue*
> *huckleberry, cobalt*
> *medicine-bottle*
> **blue.**

Shakyamuni would then be the lord of the present
world of sorrow;

> *Bhaishajyaguru*
> *Yao-Shih Fo*
> *Yakushi Nyorai,*
> *"Old Man Medicine Buddha"*

the lord of the lost paradise.
   Glory of morning,
      pearly gates, the
         heavenly blue.

Thinking on Amitabha in the setting sun.

his *western* paradise—
impurities flow out away, to east.
behind us, *rolling.*

planet ball forward turns into the "east"
is rising   azure
two thousand light-years ahead

Great Medicine Master;
land of blue.

the blue sky

the blue sky

The Blue Sky

is the land of

OLD MAN MEDICINE BUDDHA

where the eagle
that flies out of sight,

flies.

from

The
Back Country

". . . So
—when was it—I, drawn like blown
cloud, couldn't stop dreaming of
roaming, roving the coast up and
down . . ."

—Basho

Far West

A BERRY FEAST

For Joyce and Homer Matson

I

Fur the color of mud, the smooth loper
Crapulous old man, a drifter,
Praises! of Coyote the Nasty, the fat
Puppy that abused himself, the ugly gambler,
Bringer of goodies.

    In bearshit find it in August,
    Neat pile on the fragrant trail, in late
    August, perhaps by a Larch tree
    Bear has been eating the berries.
        high meadow, late summer, snow gone
    Blackbear
        eating berries, married
    To a woman whose breasts bleed
    From nursing the half-human cubs.

        Somewhere of course there are people
        collecting and junking, gibbering all day,

"Where I shoot my arrows
"There is the sunflower's shade
      —song of the rattlesnake
      coiled in the boulder's groin
"K'ak, k'ak, k'ak!
        sang Coyote. Mating with
        humankind—

        The Chainsaw falls for boards of pine,
        Suburban bedrooms, block on block
        Will waver with this grain and knot,
        The maddening shapes will start and fade
        Each morning when commuters wake—

Joined boards hung on frames,
            a box to catch the biped in.

            and shadow swings around the tree
Shifting on the berrybush
            from leaf to leaf across each day
The shadow swings around the tree.

2

Three, down, through windows
Dawn leaping cats, all barred brown, grey
Whiskers aflame
            bits of mouse on the tongue

Washing the coffeepot in the river
            the baby yelling for breakfast,
Her breasts, black-nippled, blue-veined, heavy,
Hung through the loose shirt
            squeezed, with the free hand
                white jet in three cups.
Cats at dawn
            derry derry down

Creeks wash clean where trout hide
We chew the black plug
Sleep on needles through long afternoons
            "you shall be owl
            "you shall be sparrow
            "you will grow thick and green, people
            "will eat you, you berries!
Coyote: shot from the car, two ears,
A tail, bring bounty.
    Clanks of tread
            oxen of Shang
            moving the measured road

Bronze bells at the throat
Bronze balls on the horns, the bright Oxen
Chanting through sunlight and dust
            wheeling logs down hills
                into heaps,
                        the yellow
            Fat-snout Caterpillar, tread toppling forward
Leaf on leaf, roots in gold volcanic dirt.

When
Snow melts back
            from the trees
Bare branches   knobbed pine twigs
            hot sun on wet flowers
Green shoots of huckleberry
Breaking through snow.

3

            Belly stretched taut in a bulge
            Breasts swelling as you guzzle beer, who wants
                    Nirvana?
            Here is water, wine, beer
            Enough books for a week
            A mess of afterbirth,
            A smell of hot earth, a warm mist
            Steams from the crotch

"You can't be killers all your life
"The people are coming—
        —and when Magpie
Revived him, limp rag of fur in the river
Drowned and drifting, fish-food in the shallows,
"Fuck you!" sang Coyote
                and ran.

Delicate blue-black, sweeter from meadows
Small and tart in the valleys, with light blue dust
Huckleberries scatter through pine woods
Crowd along gullies, climb dusty cliffs,
Spread through the air by birds;
Find them in droppings of bear.

"Stopped in the night
"Ate hot pancakes in a bright room
"Drank coffee, read the paper
"In a strange town, drove on,
    singing, as the drunkard swerved the car
"Wake from your dreams, bright ladies!
"Tighten your legs, squeeze demons from
    the crotch with rigid thighs
"Young red-eyed men will come
"With limp erections, snuffling cries
"To dry your stiffening bodies in the sun!

Woke at the beach. Grey dawn,
Drenched with rain. One naked man
Frying his horsemeat on a stone.

4

Coyote yaps, a knife!
Sunrise on yellow rocks.
People gone, death no disaster,
Clear sun in the scrubbed sky
                empty and bright
Lizards scurry from darkness
We lizards sun on yellow rocks.

See, from the foothills
Shred of river glinting, trailing,

To flatlands, the city:
        glare of haze in the valley horizon
Sun caught on glass gleams and goes.
From cool springs under cedar
On his haunches, white grin,
        long tongue panting, he watches:

Dead city in dry summer,
Where berries grow.

MARIN-AN

sun breaks over the eucalyptus
grove below the wet pasture,
water's about hot,
I sit in the open window
& roll a smoke.

distant dogs bark, a pair of
cawing crows; the twang
of a pygmy nuthatch high in a pine—
from behind the cypress windrow
the mare moves up, grazing.

a soft continuous roar
comes out of the far valley
of the six-lane highway—thousands
and thousands of cars
driving men to work.

SIXTH-MONTH SONG IN THE FOOTHILLS

In the cold shed sharpening saws.
      a swallow's nest hangs by the door
setting rakers in sunlight
falling from meadow through doorframe
      swallows flit under the eaves.

Grinding the falling axe
sharp for the summer
      a swallow shooting out over.
over the river, snow on low hills
sharpening wedges for splitting.

Beyond the low hills, white mountains
and now snow is melting.   sharpening tools;
      pack horses grazing new grass
bright axes—and swallows
      fly in to my shed.

THE SPRING

Beating asphalt into highway potholes
        pickup truck we'd loaded
road repair stock shed & yard
a day so hot the asphalt went in soft.
        pipe and steel plate tamper
took turns at by hand
then drive the truck rear wheel
a few times back and forth across the fill—
finish it off with bitchmo round the edge.

the foreman said let's get a drink
& drove through woods and flower fields
        shovels clattering in back
into a black grove by a cliff
        a rocked in pool
        feeding a fern ravine
                tin can to drink
numbing the hand and cramping in the gut
surging through the fingers from below
        & dark here—
let's get back to the truck
get back on the job.

A WALK

Sunday the only day we don't work:
Mules farting around the meadow,
                       Murphy fishing,
The tent flaps in the warm
Early sun: I've eaten breakfast and I'll
               take a walk
To Benson Lake. Packed a lunch,
Goodbye. Hopping on creekbed boulders
Up the rock throat three miles
             Piute Creek—
In steep gorge glacier-slick rattlesnake country
Jump, land by a pool, trout skitter,
The clear sky. Deer tracks.
Bad place by a falls, boulders big as houses,
Lunch tied to belt,
I stemmed up a crack and almost fell
But rolled out safe on a ledge
               and ambled on.
Quail chicks freeze underfoot, color of stone
Then run cheep! away, hen quail fussing.
Craggy west end of Benson Lake—after edging
Past dark creek pools on a long white slope—
Lookt down in the ice-black lake
             lined with cliff
From far above: deep shimmering trout.
A lone duck in a gunsightpass
             steep side hill
Through slide-aspen and talus, to the east end,
Down to grass, wading a wide smooth stream
Into camp. At last.
           By the rusty three-year-
Ago left-behind cookstove
Of the old trail crew,
Stoppt and swam and ate my lunch.

FIRE IN THE HOLE

Squatting a day in the sun,
    one hand turning the steeldrill,
one, swinging the four pound singlejack hammer
                    down.
three inches an hour
granite bullhump boulder
           square in the trail.
above, the cliffs,
           of Piute Mountain waver.
sweat trickles down my back.

why does this day keep coming into mind.
a job in the rock hills
    aching arms
           the muletracks
                arching blinding sky,
    noon sleep under
           snake-scale juniper limbs.

that the mind
    entered the tip of steel.
the arm fell
    like breath.
the valley, reeling,
           on the pivot of that drill—
twelve inches deep we packed the charge
    dynamite on mules
           like frankincense.
Fire in the hole!
Fire in the hole!
Fire in the hole!

jammed the plunger down.
thru dust

                     and sprinkling stone
strolld back to see:
hands and arms and shoulders
free.

BURNING THE SMALL DEAD

Burning the small dead
      branches
broke from beneath
  thick spreading
        whitebark pine.

       a hundred summers
snowmelt   rock   and air

hiss in a twisted bough.

  sierra granite;
       Mt. Ritter—
       black rock twice as old.

Deneb, Altair

windy fire

FOXTAIL PINE

bark smells like pineapple: Jeffries
cones prick your hand: Ponderosa

nobody knows what they are, saying
"needles three to a bunch."

     turpentine tin can hangers
     high lead riggers

"the true fir cone stands straight,
the doug fir cone hangs down."

—wild pigs eat acorns in those hills
cascara cutters
tanbark oak bark gatherers
myrtlewood burl bowl-makers
little cedar dolls,
      baby girl born from the split crotch
        of a plum
         daughter of the moon—

foxtail pine with a
clipped curve-back cluster of tight
    five-needle bunches
  the rough red bark scale
and jigsaw pieces sloughed off
      scattered on the ground.
—what am I doing saying "foxtail pine"?

these conifers whose home was ice
age tundra, taiga, they of the
    naked sperm
do whitebark pine and white pine seem the same?

a sort of tree
its leaves are needles
like a fox's brush
(I call him fox because he looks that way)
and call this other thing, a
foxtail pine.

AUGUST ON SOURDOUGH,
A VISIT FROM DICK BREWER

You hitched a thousand miles
                    north from San Francisco
Hiked up the mountainside   a mile in the air
The little cabin—one room—
                    walled in glass
Meadows and snowfields,   hundreds of peaks.
We lay in our sleeping bags
                    talking half the night;
Wind in the guy-cables   summer mountain rain.
Next morning I went with you
                    as far as the cliffs,
Loaned you my poncho—   the rain across the shale—
You down the snowfield
                    flapping in the wind
Waving a last goodbye   half hidden in the clouds
To go on hitching
                    clear to New York;
Me back to my mountain   and far, far, west.

OIL

soft rainsqualls on the swells
south of the Bonins, late at night. Light
from the empty mess-hall
throws back bulky shadows
of winch and fairlead
over the slanting fantail where I stand.

but for men on watch in the engine room,
the man at the wheel, the lookout in the bow,
the crew sleeps. in cots on deck
or narrow iron bunks down drumming
passageways below.

the ship burns with a furnace heart
steam veins and copper nerves
quivers and slightly twists and always goes—
easy roll of the hull and deep
vibration of the turbine underfoot.

bearing what all these
crazed, hooked nations need:
steel plates and
long injections of pure oil.

ONCE ONLY

almost at the equator
almost at the equinox
  exactly at midnight
    from a ship
      the full

    moon

in the center of the sky.

Sappa Creek near Singapore
March 1958

❧

AFTER WORK

The shack and a few trees
float in the blowing fog

I pull out your blouse,
warm my cold hands
    on your breasts.
you laugh and shudder
peeling garlic by the
    hot iron stove.
bring in the axe, the rake,
the wood

we'll lean on the wall
against each other
stew simmering on the fire
as it grows dark
      drinking wine.

FOR THE BOY WHO WAS
DODGER POINT LOOKOUT
FIFTEEN YEARS AGO

[*On a backpacking trip with my first wife in the
Olympic mountains, having crossed over from the
Dosewallips drainage, descended to and forded the
Elwha and the Goldie, and climbed again
to the high country. Hiking alone down the Elwha
from Queets basin, these years later, brings it
back.*]

The thin blue smoke of our campfire
down in the grassy, flowery,
heather meadow
two miles from your perch.
The snowmelt pond, and Alison,
half-stoopt bathing like
Swan Maiden, lovely naked,
ringed with Alpine fir and
gleaming snowy peaks. We
had come miles without trails,
you had been long alone.
We talked for half an hour up
there above the foaming creeks
and forest valleys, in our
world of snow and flowers.

I don't know where she is now;
I never asked your name.
In this burning, muddy, lying,
blood-drenched world
that quiet meeting in the mountains
cool and gentle as the muzzles of
three elk, helps keep me sane.

Far East

YASE: SEPTEMBER

Old Mrs. Kawabata
cuts down the tall spike weeds—
           more in two hours
than I can get done in a day.

out of a mountain
of grass and thistle
she saved five dusty stalks
           of ragged wild blue flower
and put them in my kitchen
               in a jar.

PINE RIVER

for Tetsu

From the top of
    Matsue castle
miles of flat ricefields
hills, and a long lake.
a schoolboy looks through a
home made telescope
    over the town.

new stores dwarf
this hilltop tower,
diving dolphins on the
    roof like horns—
nobody now quite
knows how they hoisted
    huge cut stone.

the Matsudaira family
owned it all,
sat in this windy
    lookout spire
in winter: all their
little villages
under snow.

VAPOR TRAILS

Twin streaks twice higher than cumulus,
Precise plane icetracks in the vertical blue
Cloud-flaked light-shot shadow-arcing
Field of all future war, edging off to space.

Young expert U.S. pilots waiting
The day of criss-cross rockets
And white blossoming smoke of bomb,
The air world torn and staggered for these
Specks of brushy land and ant-hill towns—

   I stumble on the cobble rockpath,
Passing through temples,
Watching for two-leaf pine
   —spotting that design.

in Daitoku-ji

THE PUBLIC BATH

the bath-girl

>   getting dressed, in the mirror,
>   the bath-girl with a pretty mole and a
>   red skirt is watching me:
>   am I
>   different?

the baby boy

>   on his back, dashed with scalding water
>   silent, moving eyes
>   inscrutably
>   pees.

the daughters

>   gripping and scrubbing his two little daughters
>   they squirm, shriek at
>   soap-in-the-eye,
>   wring out their own hair
>   with grave wifely hands,
>   peek at me, point, while he
>   soaps up and washes their
>   plump little tight-lip pussies
>   peers in their ears,
>   & dunks them in hot tile tub.
>   with a brown-burnt farmboy
>   a shrivelled old man
>   and a student who sings *silent night.*

>   —we waver and float like seaweed
>   pink flesh in the steamy light.

the old woman

    too fat and too old to care
      she just stands there
        idly knocking dewy water off her
            bush.

the young woman

    gazing vacant, drying her neck
      faint fuzz of hair
      little points of breasts
        —next year she'll be dressing
            out of sight.

the men

    squatting soapy and limber
    smooth dense skin, long muscles—

    I see dead men naked
    tumbled on beaches
        newsreels, the
          war

A VOLCANO IN KYUSHU

Mount Aso   uplands
horses, rimrock

> the sightseeing buses crammed.
> to view bare rock, brown grass,
>   space,
>   sulphury cliffs, streakt snow.
>   —whiffing the fumaroles
a noseless, shiny,
mouth-twisted middle aged man.

bluejeans, check shirt, silver buckle,
J. Robert Oppenheimer:
>   twenty years ago
>   watching the bulldozers
>   tearing down pines
>   at Los Alamos.

FOUR POEMS FOR ROBIN

Siwashing it out once in Siuslaw Forest

I slept under   rhododendron
All night   blossoms fell
Shivering on   a sheet of cardboard
Feet stuck   in my pack
Hands deep   in my pockets
Barely   able   to   sleep.
I remembered   when we were in school
Sleeping together   in a big warm bed
We were   the youngest lovers
When we broke up   we were still nineteen.
Now our   friends are married
You teach   school back east
I dont mind   living this way
Green hills   the long blue beach
But sometimes   sleeping in the open
I think back   when I had you.

A spring night in Shokoku-ji

Eight years ago this May
We walked under cherry blossoms
At night in an orchard in Oregon.
All that I wanted then
Is forgotten now, but you.
Here in the night
In a garden of the old capital
I feel the trembling ghost of Yugao
I remember your cool body
Naked under a summer cotton dress.

An autumn morning in Shokoku-ji

Last night watching the Pleiades,
Breath smoking in the moonlight,
Bitter memory like vomit
Choked my throat.
I unrolled a sleeping bag
On mats on the porch
Under thick autumn stars.
In dream you appeared
(Three times in nine years)
Wild, cold, and accusing.
I woke shamed and angry:
The pointless wars of the heart.
Almost dawn. Venus and Jupiter.
The first time I have
Ever seen them close.

December at Yase
You said, that October,
In the tall dry grass by the orchard
When you chose to be free,
"Again someday, maybe ten years."

After college I saw you
One time. You were strange.
And I was obsessed with a plan.

Now ten years and more have
Gone by: I've always known
          where you were—
I might have gone to you
Hoping to win your love back.
You still are single.

I didn't.
I thought I must make it alone. I
Have done that.

Only in dream, like this dawn,
Does the grave, awed intensity
Of our young love
Return to my mind, to my flesh.

We had what the others
All crave and seek for;
We left it behind at nineteen.

I feel ancient, as though I had
Lived many lives.

And may never now know
If I am a fool
Or have done what my
          karma demands.

THE FIRING

for Les Blakebrough and the memory of John Chappell

Bitter blue fingers
Winter nineteen sixty-three A.D.
     showa thirty-eight
Over a low pine-covered splay of hills in Shiga
West-south-west of the outlet of Lake Biwa
Domura village set on sandy fans of the sweep
     and turn of a river
Draining the rotten-granite hills up Shigaraki
On a nineteen-fifty-seven Honda cycle model C
Rode with some Yamanashi wine "St Neige"
Into the farmyard and the bellowing kiln.
Les & John
In ragged shirts and pants, dried slip
Stuck to with pineneedle, pitch,
     dust, hair, woodchips;
Sending the final slivers of yellowy pine
Through peephole white blast glow
No saggars tilting yet and segers bending
     neatly in a row—
Even their beards caked up with mud & soot
Firing for fourteen hours. How does she go.
Porcelain & stoneware: cheese dish, twenty cups.
Tokuri. vases. black chawan
Crosslegged rest on the dirt eye cockt to smoke—

The hands you layed on clay
Kickwheeld, curling,
     creamed to the lip of nothing,
And coaxt to a white dancing heat that day
Will linger centuries in these towns and loams
And speak to men or beasts
When Japanese and English
Are dead tongues.

WORK TO DO TOWARD TOWN

Venus glows in the east,
      mars hangs in the twins.
Frost on the logs and bare ground
      free of house or tree.
Kites come down from the mountains
And glide quavering over the rooftops;
      frost melts in the sun.
A low haze hangs on the houses
    —firewood smoke and mist—
Slanting far to the Kamo river
      and the distant Uji hills.
Farmwomen lead down carts
      loaded with long white radish;
I pack my bike with books—
      all roads descend toward town.

NANSEN

I found you on a rainy morning
After a typhoon
In a bamboo grove at Daitoku-ji.
Tiny wet rag with a
Huge voice, you crawled under the fence
To my hand. Left to die.
I carried you home in my raincoat.
"Nansen, cheese!" you'd shout an answer
And come running.
But you never got big,
Bandy-legged bright little dwarf—
Sometimes not eating, often coughing
Mewing bitterly at inner twinge.

Now, thin and older, you won't eat
But milk and cheese. Sitting on a pole
In the sun. Hardy with resigned
Discontent.
You just weren't made right. I saved you,
And your three-year life has been full
Of mild, steady pain.

SIX YEARS

January

        the pine tree is perfect

Walking in the snowhills the trail goes just right
Eat snow off pine needles
        the city's not so big, the
            hills surround it.
Hieizan wrapped in his own cloud—
Back there no big houses, only a little farm shack
        crows cawing back and forth
        over the valley of grass-bamboo
          and small pine.

If I had a peaceful heart it would look like this.
        the train down in the city

      was once a snowy hill

February

water taps running, the sun part out
cleaning house   sweeping floor
knocking cobwebs off the shoji   pap pap
wiping the wood and the mats with a wet rag
hands and knees on the veranda
cat-prints—make them a footwiper
                            of newspaper
wash the motorcycle.   fold clothes
start a new fire under the kama.
fill Mrs. Hosaka's kerosene stove tank,
get the cat hairs
out of the kotatsu.
take the sheets in from the bamboo poles
      where they're drying
put away the poles
stand them up below the eaves and
tie them with strings.
scrub out the floor of the bath and move the
            mirror
            and towel rack
sweep out the genkan footprints
oil the clutch cable of the motorcycle
through the oil nipple under the handle grip
      —take off sweater now because it's
            too hot
      put back on the denim jacket   work
Nansen mews angrily because he feels so sick
all the different animals are persons

what will I do about *Liberation*.
6:30 bath
charcoal.   black.   the fire part red
the ash pure white

March

Up in dirt alley
       eat korean food
drink white doboroku out of bowls
broil strips of beef & liver over coals
finish off with raw cow's womb
     in sauce, jade-white and oyster smooth
piss against the slab posts of the highways
       overhead,
bar girl girl-friend with a silver trinket cup
  hung on a neck-chain, she, gives us,
      all beer free.

sift through night streets,
Kato, Nagasawa, me, Sakaki,
okinawan awamori bar
clear glasses full up to the brim
like flavored gin—must millet—
with choppt onion.
      whirl taxi by
glass door opening sharks, their,
    eyeballs to the sky—
    in coffee, tight butt tress;
to station where the world trains meet
I south around the loop
yellow writhing dragon full of drunks
   & hall the windy concrete of
      Zojoji.

April

Firework bangs echo up the valley
   a twelve-foot snake banner
   glides off a bamboo pole at the top of a pine
two hundred people for lunch.
black umbrellas drying in the sun
—wash the red lacquer bowls
    and arrange on trays;
        cherry
    white blooms through the hilly country.

in the back right, lotus root
agé, konyaku, and a mikan.
front center sliced vinegared
   cucumber and udo.
middle, sweet red beans and
   salt yellow pickles.
front right soup
   white floating tofu
front left a tall red bowl with a bowl-like
   lid full of white steaming rice;
back left, low bowl with a round cake
   of special-fried tofu under the lid.

used trays come back
wash in heated water:
a wood tub three feet wide
drain in a five-foot basket
   on bamboo grating,
dry lacquer-ware twice and stow it in boxes
  carry them up to the
  right front corner of the white-plastered
  store house
     joined to the temple by a plank
     over the mud out back where
     corrugated iron sheets tilt
        over stacks of short firewood.

zokin in buckets of water.
wipe the long wood beams
wipe the feet of the Buddha
wipe under bronze incense stands
firecrackers boom from the shrine down the road
    five *go* of vinegar, four *go* of sugar
    five *sho* of rice;

old women half double scuttle to toilets
hoisting kimono   enroute to the door

the PA loudspeaker plays songs, plays the chants
    of the priests in the hall, the
        Dai-Hannya, Perfection
        of Wisdom

at Dragon Cloud Temple.
Five Hundred year Festival over
    they load in the busses
    or walk to their farms.

we wash ricepots, teacups, and bowls
baskets, dippers, buckets, and cauldrons,
take a bath, drink saké, and eat.
sitting on stools in the high-ceilingd kitchen

wind in the fir and the pine—
get under the quilts laid out on the mats
talk in the dark, and sleep.

May

Sitting and resting on the crest, looking far
out over Yokkawa
to a corner of Ohara—
Sugi and fir and maple on the half-logged hill

A delicate little hawk floats up
hunting delicate little country mice to eat. Lute
Lake; the noble Sugi—a tree as great as Redwood, Douglas
Fir, Sequoia, Red Cedar, Sugar Pine.

(To hell with all these cultures—history
after the Jurassic is a bore. Sugi like Sequoia;
Hinoki like a cedar)

Light wind, warm May sun & old woman bundling
brush by the trail—
men planing beams in a cool tin-roof shed
for the new Shaka-dō—fine double-edged saws
hand worn brush-hooks
battered jikatabi, funny breeches, cotton head-things
like the Navajo—
relit cigarette butts, sturdy walkers—hills and trails
of rocks and trees and people.

Quiet grey-wood copper-roofed old temple. Down
and off into the Ogi village fields, and on along
steep ridges through bamboo brush to Ohara, Jakko-in.
Jizo there with his bug-scare clanker staff

(Night ride America; thin-lipped waitress whores—)

      students listen to the tapes—
Miss Nunome in a green dress
  she usually wears something open at the neck a dab.
Yamada-kun who can't look or answer straight
  yet seems not stupid
     "A nap is 'provisional sleep' "

Blue jumper on a white blouse (Miss Yokota)
                 car honks outside

Pink fur sunset
Miss ? in a crisp white pleated skirt falling in
        precise planes–her cheeks ruddy with rouge
        "people call her 'Janie' "
        "people collar Janie"

Van Gogh print on the wall: vase of flowers all yellow
          & tawny.
Sun setting on Atago Mountain

  "strength strap strand strut struck
  strum strung strop street streak"

  "cord ford gorge dwarf forth north
  course horse doors stores dorm form
  warp sort short sport porch"

 pingpong game in the hall
Motorcycle rumbles in the streets—
horns—dark nights rain up sudden on the tin bar
         roof next door

  "try tea buy ties weigh Tim buy type
  flat tea bright ties greet Tim met Tess
  stout trap wet trip right track light tread
  high tree Joy tries gay trim fry tripe"

Why that's old Keith Lampe's voice, deep & clear

"ripples battles saddles doubled dazzled
wondered hammered eastern western southern"

Language torn up like a sewer or highway
& layed out on text
Page and tape.

July

kicking through sasa
        bear grass bamboo
            pass into thickets.
        dowse a wand knocking down spider
            net us on all sides
            sticky and strong

chirrr; semi
    hangs under   bamboo leaf

        in the heat
            sweat
    kick through sasa
snaking uphill in thickets

below, taro
    terraces down to the beach.
swim among mild red jellyfish

        a woman pickt shells, stoopt over
                    bare breasted
            kneedeep in seaweed rocks
            her two boys
                play in the tall cliff
                    shade

cross away.
     from bamboo to pinegrove
     three axes
                someone
     naps under a tree

August

night   town of lights
at sea
     unpainted rough prowed squid fishers
boats with their gas mantle lamps
miles off shore.
                counted two hundred.
                wind curls on the salt-
                sticky chest, caked ribs
     sticky sea

day dodging sun
     zigzagging barefoot
     on blistering rocks
     to dive, skim under reefs
                down along ledges
     looking for oysters or snails
                or at fish

night without blanket
sleeping on sand.
                the
     squid-fisher lights.
one-lung four-cycle engines

they sleep all day under the eaves
                headland houses
     half-naked on mats.

the wives gather shells
coarse-tongued, sun black
or working at carrying rocks
for the new coast road

   eating big lunch balls
   of cold rice.

tobacco and grapes on the dunes.
some farmers come down to the beach
in the dark   white lanterns
   sending out rowboats, swinging
a thousand-foot net
   five times down the length of the beach.
we help haul
         tumbling pockets

         glittering eyes and white bellies—
   a full-thighed young woman
   her dress tucked up in her pants
         tugs and curses
   an old man calling
   across the dark water sculling

the last haul a yard-wide ray
   she snaps off his switching
      devil-tail stinger
   & gives us three fish.

they beach their boats
full of nets
their lamps bob over the dunes

we sleep in the sand
and our salt.

September

Rucksack braced on a board, lashed tight on back,
sleeping bags, map case, tied on the gas tank
sunglasses, tennis shoes, your long tan in shorts
north on the west side of Lake Biwa
Fukui highway still being built,
        crankcase bangd on rocks—
            pusht to the very edge by a blinded truck
    I saw the sea below beside my knee:
you hung on and never knew how close.

    In Fukui found a ryokan cheap
washt off each other's dust by the square wood tub
ate dinner   on worn mats
        clean starcht yukata
        warm whisky with warm water,
all the shoji open, second floor,
        told each other
    what we'd never said before, ah,
        dallying on mats
            whispering sweat
        cools our kissing skin—

next morning rode the sunny hills, Eihei-ji,
got the luggage rack arc-welded
back through town and to the shore,
    miles-long spits and dunes of pine

and made love on the sand

The Rich have money; Give to the Rich!
   —J.C.: "All suffering is self-willed."
   you CAN take it with you
   [THE OTHERWORLD FORWARDING SERVICE
   leave your money with us;
   we'll get it through]—
Low-order Tantric phenomena.

   "God in cinders; wreck on child."

J.C.'s law—"You can't get out of the same trap
until you get into it." Hemp
   "retted" with dew or water; then the fibers
   "scutched"
Somehow life has been like . . . every day is Flag Day for me . . .
Cold turkey   with all the tremens

   [File your absence
  with NULL & VOID
    —Gilt-edged Insecurities—
  loose ends bought in vacant lots
     & the
  NOWHERE VACUUM TRUST]

     says the Armpit from Outer Space.

"1000 shares of *mikan* futures" (she's a
   Kshatriya—hell yes,
   let her run things)

Promiscuity: they sell themselves short.
     All
     Dragon-Riders

All, Dharma Kings.

November

hoeing the hataké, pull out all the clover bulb—
long white root stem, deep
    and other long roots.
"those daikon will rot in December, the frost;
    smoothing the row.
"this daikon will live through the winter.
but it don't taste so good as the other

white lime sprinkld on fresh turnd furrows like snow
these acid soils. see that daikon?
    all yellow because the ground sourd.
tiny gobo seeds, grow into twisty two foot long roots.

        spinach seeds next
soaked over night in warm water
left from the bath. makes them germinate quick.

dump weeds from the wheelbarrow back in the bamboo grove
peas planted in double rows, making holes
               four inches apart
with fore finger, stick in two seeds
            poke it in
    later fertilize all with the dippers
    yoke of wood buckets, that "human" smell
    not near so bad as you think

clean off these heavy heavy boots—
when the soil is all tilld and the winter seeds
sowed
           casts of mud
        with the back of a sickle
        stooping in gravel

December

Three a.m.—a far bell
   coming closer:
fling up useless futon on the shelf;
outside, ice-water in the hand & wash the face.
   Ko the bird-head, silent, skinny,
   swiftly cruise the room with
   salt plum tea.

Bell from the hondo chanting sutras. Gi:
deep bell, small bell, wooden drum.
   sanzen at four
   kneel on icy polisht boards in line:

Shukuza rice and pickles
barrel and bucket
dim watt bulb.
   till daybreak nap upright.
             sweep
   garden and hall.
   frost outside
         wind through walls

At eight the lecture bell. high chair.
Ke helps the robe—red, gold,
   black lacquer in the shadow
   sun and cold

Saiza a quarter to ten
soup and rice dab on the bench
feed the hungry ghosts
   back in the hall by noon.
two o clock sanzen
three o clock bellywarmer
   boild up soup-rice mush.
dinging and scuffing. out back smoke,
        and talk.

At dusk, at five,
black robes draw into the hall.
   stiff joints, sore knees bend
   the jiki pads by with his incense lit,
                      bells,
   wood block crack
& stick slips round the room
on soft straw sandals.

seven, sanzen
tea, and a leaf-shaped candy.
kinhin at eight with folded hands—
   single-file racing in flying robes leaning
           to wake—

nine o clock one more sanzen
ten, hot noodles,
three bowls each.

Sit until midnight. chant.
   make three bows and pull the futon down.
   roll in the bed—
   black.

A far bell coming closer

Envoy to Six Years

Down in the engine room again
Touching a silver steam line
    with a tiny brush.
Soogy the oil sump—gloves and rags—
—"how long you say you been Japan?
    six years eh you must like the place.
    those guys in New York
           bunch of fuckin crooks.
    they ain't just selling
    little two-bit caps, they making books."

Rinse out the soggy rag in kerosene,
And wipe off sooty oil condenser line
Driving forward geared turbine—
The driveshaft treetrunk thick,
Bearings bathed in flowing oil,

The belly of the ship.

Kali

On a corpse / dread / laughing /
four arms / a sword / a severed head /
removing fear / giving /
wearing skulls / black / naked

When I went down
to sea-lion town
my wife was dead
the canoes were gone

FOR A STONE GIRL AT SANCHI

half asleep on the cold grass
        night rain flicking the maples
under a black bowl upside-down
on a flat land
        on a wobbling speck
smaller than stars,
                space,
the size of a seed,
        hollow as bird skulls.
light flies across it
                —never is seen.

a big rock weathered funny,
old tree trunks turnd stone,
        split rocks and find clams.
                all that time
loving;
two flesh persons changing,
        clung to, doorframes
        notions, spear-hafts
in a rubble of years.
                touching,
this dream pops. it was real:
        and it lasted forever.

NORTH BEACH ALBA

waking half-drunk in a strange pad
making it out to the cool gray
    san francisco dawn—
white gulls over white houses,
    fog down the bay,
tamalpais a fresh green hill in the new sun,
driving across the bridge in a beat old car
    to work.

COULD SHE SEE THE WHOLE REAL WORLD
WITH HER GHOST BREAST EYES SHUT
UNDER A BLOUSE LID?

"A woman smells like fresh-plowed ground"
"A man smells like chewing on a maple twig"
Rockslides in the creek bed;
      picking ferns in the dark gorge.

Goldwire soft short-haired girl, one bare leg up.
Cursing the morning.
      "it's *me* there's no—"

Yellow corn woman on the way to dead-land
      by day a dead jackrabbit,
      by night a woman nursing her live baby.
Bridge of sunflower stalks.
Nursing a live baby.
                daytime, dead-land, only a hill.
Cursing the morning.
"My grandmother said they stepped single
& the hoof was split"—deer

Yellow corn girl
Blue corn girl
Squawberry flower girl

"Once a bear gets hooked on garbage there's no cure."

NIGHT

All the dark hours everywhere repair
and right the hearts & tongues of men
and makes the cheerful dawn—

the safe place in a blanket burrow
hissing in ears and nibbling wet lips
smoothing eyebrows and a stroke up the back of the knee,
licking the nape of the neck and tickling the tense
breast with fluttering eyelid, flitting
light fingers on thin chest skin,
feeling the arteries tangle the hollow groin,
arching the back backward, swinging sidewise,
      bending forward, dangling on all fours.

the bit tongue and trembling ankle,
joined palms and twined legs,
the tilted chin and beat cry,
hunched shoulders and a throb in the belly.
teeth swim in loose tongues, with toes curled.
eyes snapped shut, and quick breath.
hair all tangled together.

the radio that was never turned off.
the record soundlessly spinning.
the half-closed door swinging on its hinges.
the cigarette that burned out.
the melon seeds spit on the floor.
the mixed fluids drying on the body.
the light left on in the other room.
the blankets all thrown on the floor and the birds
      cheeping in the east.
the mouth full of grapes and the bodies like loose leaves.
the quieted hearts, passive caress, a quick exchange
      of glances with eyes then closed again,
the first sunlight hitting the shades.

THIS TOKYO

Peace, war, religion,
Revolution, will not help.
This horror seeds in the agile
Thumb and greedy little brain
That learned to catch bananas
With a stick.
     The millions of us worthless
To each other or the world
Or selves, the sufferers of the real
Or of the mind—this world
Is but a dream? Or human life
A nightmare grafted on solidity
Of planet—mental, mental,
Shudder of the sun—praise
Evil submind freedom with de Sade
Or highest Dantean radiance of the God
Or endless Light or Life or Love
Or simple tinsel angel in the
Candy heaven of the poor—
Mental divinity or beauty, all,
Plato, Aquinas, Buddha,
Dionysius of the Cross, all
Pains or pleasures hells or
What in sense or flesh
Logic, eye, music, or
Concoction of all faculties
& thought tends—tend—to this:
       This gaudy apartment of the rich.
The comfort of the U.S. for its own.
The shivering pair of girls
Who dyked each other for a show
A thousand yen before us men
—In an icy room—to buy their relatives
A meal. This scramble spawn of
Wire dirt rails tin board blocks

Babies, students, crookt old men.
    We live
On the meeting of sun and earth.
We live—we live—and all our lives
Have led to this, this city,
Which is soon the world, this
Hopelessness where love of man
Or hate of man could matter
None, love if you will or
Contemplate or write or teach
But know in your human marrow you
Who read, that all you tread
Is earthquake rot and matter mental
Trembling, freedom is a void,
Peace war religion revolution
Will not help.

27 December 56

THE MANICHAEANS

for Joanne

Our portion of fire
        at this end of the milky way
(the Tun-huang fragments say, Eternal Light)
Two million years from M 31
        the galaxy in Andromeda—
My eyes sting with these relics.
Fingers mark time.
        semen is everywhere
Two million seeds in a spurt.

Bringing hand close to your belly
        a shade off touching,
Until it feels the radiating warmth.

Your far off laughter
Is an earthquake in your thigh.
Coild like Ourabouros
        we are the Naga King
This bed is Eternal Chaos
            —and wake in a stream of light.

Cable-car cables
Whip over their greased rollers
Two feet underground.
        hemmed in by mysteries
        all moving in order.
A moment at this wide intersection,
Stoplights change, they are
        catastrophes among stars,
A red whorl of minotaurs
                gone out.
The trumpet of doom
        from a steamship at Pier 41.

Your room is cold,
          in the shade-drawn dusk inside
Light the oven, leave it open
Semi transparent jet flames rise
                    fire,
Together we make eight pounds of
Pure white mineral ash.

Your body is fossil
As you rest with your chin back
  —your arms are still flippers
                your lidded eyes lift from a swamp
Let us touch—for if two lie together
Then they have warmth.

We shall sink in this heat
              of our arms
Blankets like rock-strata fold
              dreaming as
              Shiva and Shakti
And keep back the cold.

MOTHER OF THE BUDDHAS, QUEEN OF HEAVEN, MOTHER OF THE SUN; MARICI, GODDESS OF THE DAWN

for Bhikku Ghosananda

old sow in the mud
bristles caked black
down her powerful neck

tiny hooves churn
squat body slithering
deep in food dirt

her warm filth,
deep-plowing snout,
dragging teats

those who keep her
or eat her
are cast out

she turns her small eye
from earth to
look up at me.

Nalanda, Bihar

ON OUR WAY TO KHAJURAHO

On our way to
      Khajuraho
the bus stoppt, we ate
      guavas
cheap.
        a toilet
with a picture of a woman and a man,
            two doors,
      in the square
dusty village somewhere on the way.
   a girl thirteen
      gave pice in change
to an old woman bought some sweets;
the men of Bundelkhand
wear elf-tongued
      flowery leather shoes.

she must have been low caste.
the girl stood off
      little coins
crosst from hand to hand

CIRCUMAMBULATING ARUNACHALA

for centuries sadhus live and die
in dolmen rock-slab huts near
        Arunachala

Small girls with gaudy flowers
flash down the bare walk road,
        the weight, the power,
the full warm brilliance of the human mind
        behind their eyes:
                they die or sicken in a year.

Below the hill—
wells, ponds, spiky trees,
carvd fragments of soft bodies,
        female bellies,
                centuries old.

I can't look out over cities without thinking of carpenters, plumbers, hod-carriers, cement-mixer truck drivers, plasterers

how many hours were they paid for to build up Seattle, or Portland, (which has such dark carpets—such white fir skulls—) skeleton lathe behind plaster laid on so cool—creamy under the trowel—dries to a powder, spidery lines. block bricks, shake roofs

san francisco white stairstep-up rooflines. stucco & tile houses laid out in rows in the Sunset—photos after the quake the weird frames of half-broken buildings. lunchpails in unfinished walls—how long since eyes laid on that rafter

in the hills they cast mud & fire it for rooftiles—the gray waves of Kyoto—highschool kids study their english or math in cramp ceilinged second floor rooms to the racket of looms on the ground floor, the shimmering heat of the sun-facing southward scree roof—

new buildings reinforced concrete strung full of wiring and piping, Plant in the basement—walls knock in the night—laundry ghosts chatter on flat modern roofs looking off at the shrine forest hills

the drainage of streets, hollow mountains in rows, noisy with alien molecules burning at speeds past belief, how they sift—how they clutter—

layers of mohenjo-daro, nine cities deep, a kiln at the end of the age built out in the street

forests are covered with mud and asbestos, the riverbeds sucked up and cast into plates hung on melted-down oxides

mankind your bowels are as grinding and heavy as those which forced leaves into coal, burned sand to obsidian; you draw up and lead along water, your arm rises and falls, you break through things as they are.

NANAO KNOWS

for Nanao Sakaki

Mountains, cities, all so
   light, so loose, blankets
Buckets—throw away—
Work left to do.
   it doesn't last.

Each girl is real
   her nipples harden, each has damp,
   her smell, her hair—
—What am I to be saying.
There they all go
Over the edge, dissolving.

Riveters bind up
Steel rod bundles
For wet concrete.
In and out of forests, cities, families
   like a fish.

THE TRUTH LIKE THE BELLY
OF A WOMAN TURNING

for Ali Akbar Khan

The truth
like the belly of a woman turning,
      always passes by.
      is always true.

throat and tongue—
     do we all feel the same?
     sticky hair curls

quivering throat
pitch of jaw
        strung pull
      skinnd turn, what will
    be the wrack
         of all the old—

who
cares.
    CRYING
all these passt,
       losst,
           years.

   "It always changes"
     wind child
     wound child

MOTHERS AND DAUGHTERS
   live oak and madrone.

FOR JOHN CHAPPELL

1964

Over the Arafura sea, the China sea,
    Coral sea, Pacific
chains of volcanoes in the dark—
you in Sydney where it's summer;
I imagine that last ride outward
late at night.
                stiff new gears—tight new engine
up some highway I have never seen
too fast—too fast—
    like I said at Tango
        when you went down twice on gravel—

Did you have a chance to think
o shit I've fucked it now
instant crash and flight and sudden death—

    Malaya, Indonesia
    Taiwan, the Philippines, Okinawa
        families sleeping—reaching—
        humans by the millions
        world of breathing flesh.

me in Kyoto. You in Australia
wasted in the night.
black beard, mad laugh, and sadly serious brow.
    earth lover; shaper and maker.
        potter, cooker,

    now be clay in the ground.

GO ROUND

Plunging donkey   puberty devi
   flings her thighs, swinging long
  legs backward on her mount
hair tosst
         gangle arms but eyes
           her eyes and smile are elsewhere:
swelling out and sailing to the future
  off beyond five-colord clouds.

  we enter this world trailing
       slippery clouds of guts
       incense of our flowery flesh
blossoms; crusht; re-turning
  knots of rose meat open out to—over—
  five-hued clouds—
the empty diamond of all space

And into withered, sturdy, body, stalks.
the dry branch dropping seeds.

        plunging donkey
prancing horse and trappings
  her mother watching,
      shopping bag let down
  beside her knees, against the bench,
in her eyes too the daughter
whirling
looking outward, knowing,

     having once
     steppt up on the
merry-go-
Round.

Back

THE OLD DUTCH WOMAN

The old dutch woman would spend half a day
Pacing the backyard where I lived
                    in a fixed-up shed,
What did she see.
Wet leaves, the rotten tilted-over
                over-heavy heads
Of domesticated flowers.
                    I knew Indian Paintbrush
Thought nature meant mountains,
Snowfields, glaciers and cliffs,
White granite waves underfoot.

Heian ladies
Trained to the world of the garden,
                    poetry,
    lovers slippt in with at night—

My Grandmother standing wordless
        fifteen minutes
Between rows of loganberries,
        clippers poised in her hand.

New leaves on the climbing rose
Planted last fall.
   —tiny bugs eating the green—

Like once watching
                    mountaingoats:
Far over a valley
Half into the
                    shade of the headwall,
        Pick their way over the snow.

FOR THE WEST

I

Europa,
    your red-haired
    hazel-eyed
    Thracian girls
your beautiful thighs
everlasting damnations
and grave insouciance—

a woman's country,
even your fat little popes.
            groin'd temples
            groov'd canals
—me too, I see thru
    these green eyes—

the Cowboys and Indians all over Europe
sliding down snowfields on shields.

what next? a farmer's
corner of the planet—
                  who cares if you are White?

2

this universe—"one turn"—turnd over.
      gods of revolution.
sharp beards—fur flap hats—
                kalmuck whip-swingers,

hugging and kissing
white and black,
men, men,
girls, girls,

wheat, rye, barley,
    adding asses to donkeys
    to fat-haunch horses,
it takes tractors and the
    multiple firing of pistons
to make revolution.
still turning.   flywheel heavy
      elbow-bending awkward
      flippety drive goes
on, white   chicks;

dark skin
      burns the tender lobes.
foggy white skin bleacht out,
pale nipple,
pale breast never freckled,

    they turn and
slowly turn away—

3

Ah, that's America:
the flowery glistening oil blossom
    spreading on water—
it was so tiny, nothing, now it keeps expanding
all those colors,
                    our world
    opening inside outward toward us,
each part swelling and turning
who would have thought such turning;
as it covers,
        the colors fade.
and the fantastic patterns
        fade.
I see down again through clear water.

                    ⌒

    it is the same
ball bounce rhyme the
    little girl was singing,
    all those years.

7.IV.64

up at dawn,
sweep the deck and empty garbage
chip paint down below.
all my friends have children
& I'm getting old. at least enough to be
a First Mate or an Engineer.
now I know I'll never be a Ph.D.
dumping oily buckets
in the middle of the ocean—
swirls of dried
paint drips,
white, silver, blue and green
down the outside,
full of oil—rags—
wet paint slosh coils,
marbled grease and cream.

pacific near panama

TWELVE HOURS OUT OF NEW YORK AFTER
TWENTY-FIVE DAYS AT SEA

The sun always setting behind us.
I did not mean to come this far.
　　—baseball games on the radio
　　　　commercials that turn your hair—
The last time I saild this coast
Was nineteen forty eight
Washing galley dishes
　　　reading Gide in French.
In the rucksack I've got three *nata*
Handaxes from central Japan;
The square blade found in China
　　　all the way back to Stone—
A novel by Kafu NAGAI
About geisha in nineteen-ten
With a long thing about gardens
And how they change through the year;
Azalea ought to be blooming
　　　in the yard in Kyoto now.
Now we are north of Cape Hatteras
Tomorrow docking at eight.
　　　mop the deck round the steering gear,
Pack your stuff and get paid.

19 IV 64

ACROSS LAMARCK COL

Descending hillsides in
    half morning light, step over
    small down pine,
I see myself as stony granite face.
All that we did was human,
    stupid, easily forgiven,
Not quite right.

A giving stream you give another
    should have been mine
  had I been not me
      —to whom not given—
Who most needed waited,
Stoppt off, my me,—my fault
  your black block mine—our—ours—
Myself as stony granite face—
You giving him because an   other

I also now become another.
        what I
Had not from you, for you,
        with a new lover,
Give, and give, and give, and
      take.

HOP, SKIP, AND JUMP

for Jim and Annie Hatch

the curvd lines toe-drawn, round cornerd squares
bulge out doubles from its single pillar line, like,
Venus of the Stone Age.
she takes stone,
with a white quartz band for her lagger.
                                        she
    takes a brown-staind salt-sticky cigarette
                        butt.
he takes a mussel shell. he takes a clamshell. she takes
a stick.
he is tiny, with a flying run & leap—
shaggy blond—misses all the laggers,
                tumbles from one foot.
                they are dousing
a girl in a bikini down the beach
                first with cold seawater
                then with wine.
double-leg   single-leg   stork stalk turn
on the end-square—   hop, fork, hop, scoop the lagger,
    we have all trippt and fallen.
    surf rough and full of kelp,
  all the ages—
draw a line on another stretch of sand—
                        and—
                    everybody try
to do the hop, skip, and jump.

4 X 64, Muir Beach

156

BENEATH MY HAND AND EYE THE DISTANT HILLS, YOUR BODY

What my hand follows on your body
Is the line. A stream of love
  of heat, of light,   what my
  eye   lascivious
        licks
  over, watching
  far snow-dappled Uintah mountains
Is that stream.
Of power.   what my
  hand curves over, following the line.
  "hip" and "groin"
Where "I"
  follow by hand and eye
  the swimming limit of your body.
As when vision idly dallies on the hills
Loving what it feeds on.
  soft cinder cones and craters;
    —Drum Hadley in the Pinacate
      took ten minutes more to look again—
A leap of power unfurling:
    left,   right—right—
My heart beat faster looking
  at the snowy Uintah mountains.

As my hand feeds on you
  runs down your side and curls beneath your hip.
  oil pool; stratum; water—

What "is" within   not known
  but feel it
  sinking with a breath
  pusht ruthless, surely, down.

Beneath this long caress of hand and eye
  "we" learn the flower burning,
        outward, from "below".

THROUGH THE SMOKE HOLE

for Don Allen

I

There is another world above this one; or outside of this one; the way to it is thru the smoke of this one, & the hole that smoke goes through. The ladder is the way through the smoke hole; the ladder holds up, some say, the world above; it might have been a tree or pole; I think it is merely a way.

Fire is at the foot of the ladder. The fire is in the center. The walls are round. There is also another world below or inside this one. The way there is down thru smoke. It is not necessary to think of a series.

Raven and Magpie do not need the ladder. They fly thru the smoke holes shrieking and stealing. Coyote falls thru; we recognize him only as a clumsy relative, a father in old clothes we don't wish to see with our friends.

It is possible to cultivate the fields of our own world without much thought for the others. When men emerge from below we see them as the masked dancers of our magic dreams. When men disappear down, we see them as plain men going somewhere else. When men disappear up we see them as great heroes shining through the smoke. When men come back from above they fall thru and tumble; we don't really know them; Coyote, as mentioned before.

II

Out of the kiva come
masked dancers or
plain men.
    plain men go into the ground.

out there out side all the chores
   wood and water, dirt,
wind, the view across the flat,
here, in the round
              no corners
head is full of magic figures—
woman your secrets aren't my secrets
what I cant say I wont
walk round
put my hand flat down.
you in the round too.
gourd vine blossom.
walls and houses drawn up
from the same soft soil.

thirty million years gone
      drifting sand.
  cool rooms pink stone
worn down fort floor, slat sighting
  heat shine on jumna river

dry wash, truck tracks in the riverbed
coild sand pinyon.

     seabottom
     riverbank
     sand dunes
the floor of a sea once again.

                 human fertilizer
                 underground water tunnels
                 skinny dirt gods
                 grandmother berries
                                        out
through the smoke hole.
      (for childhood and youth *are* vanity)

a Permian reef of algae,

out through the smoke hole
swallowd sand
               salt mud
swum bodies,   flap
to the limestone blanket—

lizzard tongue,   lizzard tongue

      wha, wha, wha   flying
in and *out* thru the smoke hole

               plain men
      come out of the ground.

For Masa

from

Regarding Wave

WAVE

Grooving clam shell,
        streakt through marble,
      sweeping down ponderosa pine bark-scale
        rip-cut tree grain
              sand-dunes, lava
                 flow

Wave   wife.
        woman—wyfman—
"veiled; vibrating; vague"
  sawtooth ranges pulsing;
                 veins on the back of the hand.

Forkt out: birdsfoot-alluvium
             wash

       great dunes rolling
Each inch rippld, every grain a wave.

Leaning against sand cornices til they blow away

   —wind, shake
   stiff thorns of cholla, ocotillo
   sometimes I get stuck in thickets—

Ah, trembling spreading radiating wyf
            racing zebra
  catch me and fling me wide
To the dancing grain of things
           of my mind!

IN THE HOUSE OF THE RISING SUN

Skinny kids in shorts get cups
    full of rice-gruel—steaming
    breakfast—sling
    their rifles, walk
    hot thickets.
    eyes peeled for U S planes.

Kyoto   a bar girl in pink
    with her catch for the night
    —but it's already morning—half-
    dazed, neat suit,
    laugh toward bed,

A guy I worked at logging with in Oregon
    fiddles his new lead-belcher cannons
        in South Yüeh.
    tuned better than chainsaws,
      at dawn,
    he liked mush.   with raisins.

Sleeping out   all night
   in warm rain.
Viet Nam uplands burned-off jungles
   wipe out a few rare birds
Fish in the rice paddy ditches
   stream a dry foul taste thru their gills
New Asian strains of clap
   whip penic   ill in.

Making toast, heating coffee,
    blue as Shiva—
    did I drink some filthy poison
    will I ever learn to love?

Did I really have to kill my sick, sick cat.

SONG OF THE TANGLE

Two thigh hills hold us at the fork
        round mount center

        we sit all folded
on the dusty planed planks of a shrine
drinking top class saké that was left
        for the god.

        calm tree halls
        the sun past the summit
        heat sunk through the vines,
            twisted sasa

        cicada singing,
            swirling in the tangle

the tangle of the thigh

        the brush
        through which we push

SONG OF THE SLIP

SLEPT
folded in girls
feeling their folds; whorls;
the lips, leafs,
of the curling   soft-sliding
serpent-sleep dream.

roaring and faring
to beach high on the dark shoal
seed-prow

moves in and makes home in the whole.

SONG OF THE TASTE

Eating the living germs of grasses
Eating the ova of large birds

   the fleshy sweetness packed
   around the sperm of swaying trees

The muscles of the flanks and thighs of
           soft-voiced cows
   the bounce in the lamb's leap
   the swish in the ox's tail

Eating roots grown swoll
       inside the soil

Drawing on life of living
   clustered points of light spun
       out of space
hidden in the grape.

Eating each other's seed
       eating
  ah, each other.

Kissing the lover in the mouth of bread:
      lip to lip.

KYOTO BORN IN SPRING SONG

Beautiful little children
     found in melons,
     in bamboo,
   in a "strangely glowing warbler egg"
     a perfect baby girl—

baby, baby,
  tiny precious
     mice and worms:

  Great majesty of Dharma turning
  Great dance of Vajra power

lizard baby by the fern
centipede baby scrambling toward the wall
cat baby left to mew for milk alone
mouse baby too afraid to run

     O sing   born in spring
  the weavers swallows babies in Nishijin
     nests below the eaves

     glinting mothers wings
     swoop to the sound of looms

    and three fat babies
  with three human mothers
every morning doing laundry
          "good
morning how's your baby?"
Tomoharu, Itsuko, and Kenji—

   Mouse, begin again.

Bushmen are laughing
   at the coyote-tricking
        that made us think machines

   wild babies
in the ferns and plums and weeds.

BURNING ISLAND

O Wave God   who broke through me today
    Sea Bream
    massive pink and silver
    cool swimming down with me watching
                staying away from the spear

Volcano belly Keeper who lifted this island
    for our own beaded bodies adornment
    and sprinkles us all with his laugh—
             ash in the eye
    mist, or smoke,
    on the bare high limits—
             underwater lava flows easing to coral
                 holes filled with striped feeding swimmers

O Sky Gods   cartwheeling
    out of   Pacific
    turning rainsqualls over like lids on us
    then shine on our sodden—
             (scanned out a rainbow today at the
                cow drinking trough
                   sluicing off
        LAKHS of crystal Buddha Fields
       right on the hair of the arm!)

Who wavers right now in the bamboo:
  a half-gone waning moon.
             drank down a bowlful of shochu
               in praise of Antares
               gazing far up the lanes of Sagittarius
               richest stream of our sky—
  a cup to the center of the galaxy!
             and let the eyes stray
  right-angling the pitch of the Milky Way:
             horse-heads   rings

clouds   too distant to *be*
slide free.
        on the crest of the wave.

Each night
O Earth Mother
  I have wrappt my hand
  over the jut of your cobra-hood
             sleeping;
  left my ear
All night long by your mouth.

O   All
Gods tides capes currents
Flows and spirals of
    pool and powers—

As we hoe the field
  let sweet potato grow.
And as sit us all down when we may
To consider the Dharma
  bring with a flower and a glimmer.
Let us all sleep in peace   together.

Bless Masa and me as we marry
  at new moon   on the crater
This summer.

VIII 40067

ROOTS

Draw over and dig
The loose ash soil
Hoe handles are short,
The sun's course long
Fingers deep in the earth search
Roots, pull them out; feel through;
Roots are strong.

RAINBOW BODY

Cicada fill up the bamboo thickets:
  a wall of twanging shadow
    dark joints and leaves.
         northwest wind
    from the China sea.

Salt clouds skim the volcano
   mixed with ash and steam
     rumbles downwind
         from the night gleam
    summit, near Algol,
  breathing the Milky Way.

The great drone
In the throat of the hill
The waves drum
The wind sigh.

At dawn the mountain canyons
   spread and rise
  to the falling call of the Akahige
     we half-wake
         in the east light
    fresh

At low tide swim out through a path in the coral
  & into the land of the sea-people:
  rainbows under the foam of the breakers
     surge and streaming

                    from the southern beach.
           the lips, where you float
           clear, wave
           with the subtle currents
           sea-tangle tendrils
outward roil of lava
                —cobalt speckled curling
           mouth of a *shako* clam.

Climb delicately back up the cliff
     without using our hands.
     eat melon and steamed sweet potato
     from this ground.
We hoed and fished—
     grubbing out bamboo runners
     hammering straight blunt
     harpoon heads and spears
                Now,
           sleep on the cliff
           float on the surf
           nap in the bamboo thicket
                eyes closed,
           dazzled ears.

EVERYBODY LYING ON THEIR STOMACHS, HEAD TOWARD THE CANDLE, READING, SLEEPING, DRAWING

The corrugated roof
Booms and fades night-long to

million-darted rain
squalls   and

outside

lightning

Photographs in the brain
Wind-bent bamboo.
through

the plank shutter
set

Half-open   on eternity

SHARK MEAT

In the night fouled the nets—
Sonoyama's flying-fish fishing
Speared by the giant trident
        that hung in the net shed
        we never thought used

Cut up for meat on the beach.
At seven in the morning
Maeda's grandson
        the shy one
        —a slight harelip
Brought a crescent of pale red flesh
        two feet long, looped on his arm
Up the bamboo lanes to our place.

The island eats shark meat at noon.

Sweet miso sauce on a big boiled cube
        as I lift a flake

                to my lips,

Miles of water, Black current,
Thousands of days
        re-crossing his own paths
        to tangle our net
            to be part of
            this loom.

THE BED IN THE SKY

Motorcycle strums   the empty streets
Heading home at one a.m.
    ice slicks shine in the moon
                I weave a safe path through

Naked shivering light flows down
Fills the basin over Kyoto
        and the plain
                a ghost glacier dream

From here a hundred miles are clear
The cemetery behind
        Namu   Amida   Butsu
                chiselled   ten thousand times

Tires crackle the mud-puddles
The northern hills gleam white
        I ought to stay outside   alone
                and watch the moon all night

But the bed is full and spread and dark
I hug you and sink in the warm
        my stomach against your big belly

            feels our baby turn

KAI, TODAY

A teen-age boy in training pants
      stretching by the river
A girl child weeping, climbing
      up her elder sister;
The Kawaramachi Beggar's steady look and
      searching reach of gritty hand
      in plastic sidewalk pail
         with lip of grease

      these fates.

      before Masa and I met
What's your from-the-beginning face?
      Kai.
      born again
To the Mother's hoarse bear-down
      groan and dark red mask:
      spiralling, glistening, blue-white, up

And out from her
        (dolphins leaping in threes
        through blinding silver inter-
        faces, Persian
        Gulf tanker's wave-slip
        opening, boundless
         whap
      as they fall back,
      arcing
      into her—)

      sea.

NOT LEAVING THE HOUSE

When Kai is born
I quit going out

Hang around the kitchen—make cornbread
Let nobody in.
Mail is flat.
    Masa lies on her side, Kai sighs,
    Non washes and sweeps
We sit and watch
    Masa nurse, and drink green tea.

Navajo turquoise beads over the bed
A peacock tail feather at the head
A badger pelt from Nagano-ken
For a mattress; under the sheet;
A pot of yogurt setting
Under the blankets, at his feet.

Masa, Kai,
And Non, our friend
In the green garden light reflected in
Not leaving the house.
From dawn til late at night
    making a new world of ourselves
    around this life.

REGARDING WAVE

The voice of the Dharma
    the voice
      now

A shimmering bell
    through all.

Every hill,   still.
Every tree alive. Every leaf.
All the slopes   flow.
      old woods, new seedlings,
      tall grasses plumes.

Dark hollows;   peaks of light.
  wind stirs   the cool side
Each leaf living.
      All the hills.

      The Voice
      is a wife
        to

      him still.

    ōm   ah   hūm

REVOLUTION IN THE REVOLUTION
IN THE REVOLUTION

The country surrounds the city
The back country surrounds the country

"From the masses to the masses" the most
Revolutionary consciousness is to be found
Among the most ruthlessly exploited classes:
Animals, trees, water, air, grasses

We must pass through the stage of the
"Dictatorship of the Unconscious" before we can
Hope for the withering-away of the states
And finally arrive at true Communionism.

∾

If the capitalists and imperialists
   are the exploiters, the masses are the workers.
     and the party
     is the communist.

If civilization
   is the exploiter, the masses is nature.
     and the party
     is the poets.

If the abstract rational intellect
   is the exploiter, the masses is the unconscious.
     and the party
     is the yogins.

& POWER
comes out of the seed-syllables of mantras.

WHAT YOU SHOULD KNOW TO BE A POET

all you can about animals as persons.
the names of trees and flowers and weeds.
names of stars, and the movements of the planets
                    and the moon.

your own six senses, with a watchful and elegant mind.

at least one kind of traditional magic:
divination, astrology, the *book of changes,* the tarot;

dreams.
the illusory demons and illusory shining gods;

kiss the ass of the devil and eat shit;
fuck his horny barbed cock,
fuck the hag,
and all the celestial angels
                    and maidens perfum'd and golden—

& then love the human: wives   husbands   and friends.

children's games, comic books, bubble-gum,
the weirdness of television and advertising.

work, long dry hours of dull work swallowed and accepted
and livd with and finally lovd.   exhaustion,
                    hunger, rest.

the wild freedom of the dance, *extasy*
silent solitary illumination, *enstasy*

real danger.   gambles.   and the edge of death.

AGED TAMBA TEMPLE PLUM TREE SONG

Firewood under the eaves
    ends trimm'd even

Scaly silver lichen
    on the plum
        bark
Ragged, rough, twisted,
    parts half-rotted

A few blossoms open:
    rich pink tiny petals
        soft and flutter;
Other fat buds.

Fat buds, green twigs,
    flaky gray bark;

        pigeons must all
Flap up together

IT

*[Reading Blake in a cowshed during a
typhoon on an island in the East China Sea]*

Cloud—cloud—cloud—   hurls
      up and on over;
Bison herds stamp-
peding   on Shantung

Fists of rain
      flail half down the length of the floor
Bamboo hills
      bend and regain;
            fields follow the laws of waves.

      puppy scuds in wet
      squats on the slat bed
            —on the edge of a spiral
Centered five hundred miles southwest.

Reading in English:
      the way the words join
      the weights, the warps,

      I know   what it means.
      my language is home.

            mind-fronts meeting
            bite back at each other,
            whirl up a Mother Tongue.
      one hundred knot gusts dump palms
      over somebody's morning cream—

Cowshed skull
Its windows open
      swallows and strains
      gulfs of wild-slung
            quivering ocean air.
            breathe it;
            taste it;   how it

Feeds the brain.

RUNNING WATER MUSIC

under the trees
under the clouds
by the river
on the beach,

"sea roads."
whales   great sea-path beasts—

         salt;   cold
         water;   smoky fire.
steam, cereal,
         stone, wood boards.
bone awl, pelts,
         bamboo pins and spoons.
unglazed bowl.
a band around the hair.

       beyond wounds.

sat on a rock in the sun,
watched the old pine
wave
over blinding fine white
         river sand.

SOURS OF THE HILLS

barbed seeds   in double ranks
sprung for sending off;

half-moon hairy seeds in the hair of the wrist

majestic fluff
sails . . . rayed and spined. . .up hill at eye level
    hardly a breeze;

amber fruit with veins
on a bending stem,
size of an infant pea.

plumes wave,
seeds spill.

blueblack berry on a bush turned leaf-purple

deep sour, dark tart, sharp
    in the back of the mouth.

in the hair and from head to foot
stuck with seeds—burrs—
    next summer's mountain weeds—

a strolling through vines and grasses:

into the wild sour.

THE WILD EDGE

Curve of the two steel spring-up prongs on
      the back of the Hermes
        typewriter—paper holders—the same
Curve as the arched wing of a gull:

        (sails through the
      sides of the eyes by white-stained cliffs
      car-park lots and scattered
        pop-top beer tabs in the gravel)

Birds sail away and back.

Sudden flurry and buzz of flies in the corner sun.
Heavy beetle drags stiff legs through moss

Caravans of ants bound for the Wall
        wandering backward—

Harsh Thrush shrieks   in the cherries.
      a murmur in the kitchen
     Kai wakes and cries—

THE TRADE

I found myself inside a massive concrete shell
    lit by glass tubes, with air pumped in, with
    levels joined by moving stairs.

It was full of the things that were bought and made
    in the twentieth century. Layed out in trays
    or shelves

The throngs of people of that century, in their style,
    clinging garb made on machines,

Were trading all their precious time
    for things.

TO FIRE

(Goma / Homa)

I have raised pure flames
With mystic fists and muttered charms!

All the poems I wrote before nineteen
Heaps of arty cards from Christmas
Straw shoes
Worn clogs
The English Daily—Johnson's, Wilson's Ho Chi Minh
    —face crumpling inward licked by yellow locks

The contracting writhing plastics
And orange skins that shrink and squeak
                peace! peace! grace!

Using sanctified vajra-tongs of blue
I turn the mass and let in air

Those letters forwarded now to Shiva
the knots of snot in kleenex,
              my offering—my body!

And here the drafts of articles and songs
Words of this and that

Bullshit—renounce
            the leather briefcase no one wants
            the holey socks.

As sun moves up and up;
And motorcycles warm the street;

And people at the bus stop steam—

GREAT BRILLIANT KING
Unshakeable!
—halo of flame—
Eat   these   sweets   of   our   house   and   day   :

Let me unflinching burn
Such dross within
With joy
I pray!

LOVE

Women who were turned inside-out
Ten times over by childbirth

On the wind-washed lonely islands
Lead the circle of *obon* dancers
Through a full moon night in August

The youngest girl last;

Women who were up since last night
Scaling and cleaning the flying fish

Sing about love.

Over and over,
Sing about love.

Suwa-no-se Island

MEETING THE MOUNTAINS

He crawls to the edge of the foaming creek
He backs up the slab ledge
He puts a finger in the water
He turns to a trapped pool
Puts both hands in the water
Puts one foot in the pool
Drops pebbles in the pool
He slaps the water surface with both hands
He cries out, rises up and stands
Facing toward the torrent and the mountain
Raises up both hands and shouts three times!

VI 69, Kai at Sawmill Lake

RUNNING WATER MUSIC II

Clear running stream
       clear running stream

Your water is light
       to my mouth
And a light to my dry body

       your flowing
Music,
       in my ears. free,

Flowing free!
With you
       in me.

LONG HAIR

Hunting season:

Once every year, the Deer catch human beings. They
do various things which irresistibly draw men near them;
each one selects a certain man. The Deer shoots the man,
who is then compelled to skin it and carry its meat home
and eat it. Then the Deer is inside the man. He waits
and hides in there, but the man doesn't know it. When
enough Deer have occupied enough men, they will strike
all at once. The men who don't have Deer in them will
also be taken by surprise, and everything will change
some. This is called "takeover from inside."

Deer trails:

Deer trails run on the side hills
        cross county access roads
        dirt ruts to bone-white
        board house ranches,
        tumbled down.

Waist high through manzanita,
Through sticky, prickly, crackling
        gold dry summer grass.

Deer trails lead to water,
Lead sidewise all ways
Narrowing down to one best path—
And split—
And fade away to nowhere.

Deer trails slide under freeways
        slip into cities

swing back and forth in crops and orchards
run up the sides of schools!

Deer spoor and crisscross dusty tracks
Are in the house: and coming out the walls:

And deer bound through my hair.

TARGET PRACTICE

FOR WILL PETERSEN THE TIME WE CLIMBED MT. HIEI
CROSS-COUNTRY IN THE SNOW

No trail
    can't be followed:
        wild boar tracks slash
        sidehill through bamboo
                  thicket.
Where are we   the hill
Goes up.

                    ❧

    ranges of hazy hills
    make the heart ache—
tiny flowers in the underbrush,
    winds from Siberia
               in the spring.

                    ❧

WHY I LAUGH WHEN KAI CRIES

Nothing's to blame:
    daily hunger, baby rage—
            the Buddha's Lion Roar
            and hymns of praise.

Belly and nerves,
    floating gathering mind
            feel pain and wail
            he's getting fat
I have to laugh at that.

SOME GOOD THINGS TO BE SAID FOR THE IRON AGE

A ringing tire iron
        dropped on the pavement

Whang of a saw
brusht on limbs

                the taste
                of rust.

CIVILIZATION

Those are the people who do complicated things.

    they'll grab us by the thousands
    and put us to work.
World's going to hell, with all these
    villages and trails.
Wild duck flocks aren't
    what they used to be.
Aurochs grow rare.

Fetch me my feathers and amber

A small cricket
on the typescript page of

"Kyoto born in spring song"
grooms himself
in time with *The Well-Tempered Clavier.*
I quit typing and watch him thru a glass.
How well articulated! How neat!

Nobody understands the ANIMAL KINGDOM.

❧

When creeks are full
The poems flow
When creeks are down
We heap stones.

For Lois Snyder Hennessy
my mother

from

Turtle
Island

INTRODUCTORY NOTE

Turtle Island—the old/new name for the continent, based on many creation myths of the people who have been living here for millennia, and reapplied by some of them to "North America" in recent years. Also, an idea found world-wide, of the earth, or cosmos even, sustained by a great turtle or serpent-of-eternity.

A name: that we may see ourselves more accurately on this continent of watersheds and life-communities—plant zones, physiographic provinces, culture areas: following natural boundaries. The "U.S.A." and its states and counties are arbitrary and inaccurate impositions on what is really here.

The poems speak of place, and the energy-pathways that sustain life. Each living being is a swirl in the flow, a formal turbulence, a "song." The land, the planet itself, is also a living being—at another pace. Anglos, Black people, Chicanos, and others beached up on these shores all share such views at the deepest levels of their old cultural traditions—African, Asian, or European. Hark again to those roots, to see our ancient solidarity, and then to the work of being together on Turtle Island.

Manzanita

ANASAZI

Anasazi,
Anasazi,

tucked up in clefts in the cliffs
growing strict fields of corn and beans
sinking deeper and deeper in earth
up to your hips in Gods
        your head all turned to eagle-down
        & lightning for knees and elbows
your eyes full of pollen

        the smell of bats.
        the flavor of sandstone
        grit on the tongue.

        women
        birthing
at the foot of ladders in the dark.

trickling streams in hidden canyons
under the cold rolling desert

corn-basket   wide-eyed
        red baby
        rock lip home,

Anasazi

THE WAY WEST, UNDERGROUND

The split-cedar
smoked salmon
cloudy days of Oregon,
the thick fir forests.

      Black Bear heads uphill in
      Plumas county,
      round bottom scuttling through willows—

The Bear Wife moves up the coast.

      where blackberry brambles
      ramble in the burns.

And around the curve of islands
foggy volcanoes
on, to North Japan. The bears
& fish-spears of the Ainu.
Gilyak.
Mushroom-vision healer,
single flat drum,
from long before China.

Women with drums who fly over Tibet.

Following forests west, and
rolling, following grassland,
tracking bears and mushrooms,
eating berries all the way.
In Finland finally took a bath:
      like redwood sweatlodge on the Klamath—
all the Finns in moccasins and
pointy hats with dots of white,
netting, trapping, bathing,
singing holding hands, the while

see-sawing on a bench, a look of love—

Karhu—Bjorn—Braun—Bear

        [lightning rainbow great cloud tree
             dialogs of birds]
Europa.   'The West.'
the bears are gone
           except Brunhilde?

Or elder wilder goddesses reborn—will race
   the streets of France and Spain
        with automatic guns—
        in Spain,
Bears and Bison,
Red Hands with missing fingers,
red mushroom labyrinths;
lightning-bolt mazes,
painted in caves,

underground.

THE DEAD BY THE SIDE OF THE ROAD

How did a great Red-tailed Hawk
   come to lie—all stiff and dry—
      on the shoulder of
            Interstate 5?

Her wings for dance fans

Zac skinned a skunk with a crushed head
   washed the pelt in gas; it hangs,
      tanned, in his tent

Fawn stew on Hallowe'en
   hit by a truck on highway forty-nine
      offer cornmeal by the mouth;
         skin it out.

Log trucks run on fossil fuel

I never saw a Ringtail til I found one in the road:
   case-skinned it with the toenails
      footpads, nose, and whiskers on;
         it soaks in salt and water
         sulphuric acid pickle;

she will be a pouch for magic tools.

The Doe was apparently shot
   lengthwise and through the side—
      shoulder and out the flank
         belly full of blood

Can save the other shoulder maybe,
   if she didn't lie too long—

Pray to their spirits. Ask them to bless us:
   our ancient sisters' trails
      the roads were laid across and kill them:
         night-shining eyes

The dead by the side of the road.

I WENT INTO THE MAVERICK BAR

I went into the Maverick Bar
In Farmington, New Mexico.
And drank double shots of bourbon
                    backed with beer.
My long hair was tucked up under a cap
I'd left the earring in the car.

Two cowboys did horseplay
                    by the pool tables,
A waitress asked us
                    where are you from?
a country-and-western band began to play
"We don't smoke Marijuana in Muskokie"
And with the next song,
                    a couple began to dance.

They held each other like in High School dances
                    in the fifties;
I recalled when I worked in the woods
                    and the bars of Madras, Oregon.
That short-haired joy and roughness—
                    America—your stupidity.
I could almost love you again.

We left—onto the freeway shoulders—
                    under the tough old stars—
In the shadow of bluffs
                    I came back to myself,
To the real work, to
                    "What is to be done."

Karl Marx?

NO MATTER, NEVER MIND

The Father is the Void
The Wife   Waves

Their child is Matter.

Matter makes it with his mother
And their child is Life,
                      a daughter.

The Daughter is the Great Mother
Who, with her father/brother Matter
                    as her lover,

Gives birth to the Mind.

THE BATH

about relationships
"our" body

Washing Kai in the sauna,
The kerosene lantern set on a box
    outside the ground-level window,
Lights up the edge of the iron stove and the
    washtub down on the slab
Steaming air and crackle of waterdrops
    brushed by on the pile of rocks on top
He stands in warm water
Soap all over the smooth of his thigh and stomach
    "Gary don't soap my hair!"
    —his eye-sting fear—
    the soapy hand feeling
    through and around the globes and curves of his body
    up in the crotch,
And washing-tickling out the scrotum, little anus,
    his penis curving up and getting hard
    as I pull back skin and try to wash it
Laughing and jumping, flinging arms around,
    I squat all naked too,
                        is this our body?

Sweating and panting in the stove-steam hot-stone
    cedar-planking wooden bucket water-splashing
    kerosene lantern-flicker wind-in-the-pines-out
    sierra forest ridges night—
Masa comes in, letting fresh cool air
    sweep down from the door
    a deep sweet breath
And she tips him over gripping neatly, one knee down
    her hair falling hiding one whole side of
    shoulder, breast, and belly,
Washes deftly Kai's head-hair
    as he gets mad and yells—
The body of my lady, the winding valley spine,
    the space between the thighs I reach through,

cup her curving vulva arch and hold it from behind,
      a soapy tickle   a hand of grail
The gates of Awe
That open back a turning double-mirror world of
      wombs in wombs, in rings,
      that start in music,
                        is this our body?

The hidden place of seed
The veins net flow across the ribs, that gathers
      milk and peaks up in a nipple—fits
      our mouth—
The sucking milk from this our body sends through
      jolts of light; the son, the father,
      sharing mother's joy
That brings a softness to the flower of the awesome
      open curling lotus gate I cup and kiss
As Kai laughs at his mother's breast he now is weaned
      from, we
      wash each other,
                        this our body

Kai's little scrotum up close to his groin,
      the seed still tucked away, that moved from us to him
In flows that lifted with the same joys forces
      as his nursing Masa later,
      playing with her breast,
Or me within her,
Or him emerging,
                        this is our body:

Clean, and rinsed, and sweating more, we stretch
      out on the redwood benches hearts all beating
Quiet to the simmer of the stove,
      the scent of cedar
And then turn over,
      murmuring gossip of the grasses,
      talking firewood,

Wondering how Gen's napping, how to bring him in
    soon wash him too—
These boys who love their mother
    who loves men, who passes on
    her sons to other women;

The cloud across the sky. The windy pines.
    the trickle gurgle in the swampy meadow

    this is our body.

Fire inside and boiling water on the stove
We sigh and slide ourselves down from the benches
    wrap the babies, step outside,

black night & all the stars.

Pour cold water on the back and thighs
Go in the house—stand steaming by the center fire
Kai scampers on the sheepskin
Gen standing hanging on and shouting,

"Bao! bao! bao! bao! bao!"

This is our body. Drawn up crosslegged by the flames
    drinking icy water
    hugging babies, kissing bellies,

Laughing on the Great Earth

Come out from the bath.

SPEL AGAINST DEMONS

The release of Demonic Energies in the name of
                    the People
          must cease

Messing with blood sacrifice in the name of
                    Nature
          must cease

The stifling self-indulgence in anger in the name of
                    Freedom
          must cease

this is death to clarity
death to compassion

the man who has the soul of the wolf
knows the self-restraint
of the wolf

aimless executions and slaughterings
are not the work of wolves and eagles

but the work of hysterical sheep

The Demonic must be devoured!
Self-serving must be
                    cut down
Anger must be
                    plowed back
Fearlessness, humor, detachment, is power

Gnowledge is the secret of Transformation!

Down with demonic killers who mouth revolutionary
slogans and muddy the flow of change, may they be

Bound by the Noose, and Instructed by the Diamond
Sword of ACHALA the Immovable, Lord of Wisdom, Lord
of Heat, who is squint-eyed and whose face is terrible
with bare fangs, who wears on his crown a garland of
severed heads, clad in a tiger skin, he who turns
Wrath to Purified Accomplishment,

    whose powers are of lava,
    of magma, of deep rock strata, of gunpowder,
             and the Sun.

He who saves tortured intelligent demons and filth-eating
        hungry ghosts, his spel is,

NAMAH SAMANTAH VAJRANAM CHANDA
  MAHAROSHANA
        SPHATAYA HUM TRAKA HAM MAM

uses of anger?

FRONT LINES

The edge of the cancer
Swells against the hill—we feel
         a foul breeze—
And it sinks back down.
The deer winter here
A chainsaw growls in the gorge.

Ten wet days and the log trucks stop,
The trees breathe.
Sunday the 4-wheel jeep of the
Realty Company brings in
Landseekers, lookers, they say
To the land,
Spread your legs.

The jets crack sound overhead, it's OK here;
Every pulse of the rot at the heart
In the sick fat veins of Amerika
Pushes the edge up closer—

A bulldozer grinding and slobbering
Sideslipping and belching on top of
The skinned-up bodies of still-live bushes
In the pay of a man
From town.

Behind is a forest that goes to the Arctic
And a desert that still belongs to the Piute
And here we must draw
Our line.

CONTROL BURN

What the Indians
here
used to do, was,
to burn out the brush every year.
in the woods, up the gorges,
keeping the oak and the pine stands
tall and clear
with grasses
and kitkitdizze under them,
never enough fuel there
that a fire could crown.

Now, manzanita,
(a fine bush in its right)
crowds up under the new trees
mixed up with logging slash
and a fire can wipe out all.

Fire is an old story.
I would like,
with a sense of helpful order,
with respect for laws
of nature,
to help my land
with a burn. a hot clean
burn.
       (manzanita seeds will only open
       after a fire passes over
       or once passed through a bear)

And then
it would be more
like,
when it belonged to the Indians

Before.

THE CALL OF THE WILD

The heavy old man in his bed at night
Hears the Coyote singing
                in the back meadow.
All the years he ranched and mined and logged.
A Catholic.
A native Californian.
        and the Coyotes howl in his
Eightieth year.
He will call the Government
Trapper
Who uses iron leg-traps on Coyotes,
Tomorrow.
My sons will lose this
Music they have just started
To love.

                              ꙮ

The ex acid-heads from the cities
Converted to Guru or Swami,
Do penance with shiny
Dopey eyes, and quit eating meat.
In the forests of North America,
The land of Coyote and Eagle,
They dream of India, of
        forever blissful sexless highs.
And sleep in oil-heated
Geodesic domes, that
Were stuck like warts
In the woods.

And the Coyote singing
        is shut away
        for they fear

the call
of the wild.

And they sold their virgin cedar trees,
    the tallest trees in miles,
To a logger
Who told them,

"Trees are full of bugs."

The Government finally decided
To wage the war   all-out. Defeat
    is Un-American.
And they took to the air,
Their women beside them
    in bouffant hairdos
    putting nail-polish on the
    gunship cannon-buttons.
And they never came down,
    for they found,
    the ground
is pro-Communist. And dirty.
And the insects side with the Viet Cong.

So they bomb and they bomb
Day after day, across the planet
    blinding sparrows
    breaking the ear-drums of owls
    splintering trunks of cherries
    twining and looping
    deer intestines
    in the shaken, dusty, rocks.

All these Americans up in special cities in the sky
Dumping poisons and explosives

Across Asia first,
And next North America,

A war against earth.
When it's done there'll be
     no place

A Coyote could hide.

envoy

I would like to say
Coyote is forever
Inside you.

But it's not true.

PRAYER FOR THE GREAT FAMILY

Gratitude to Mother Earth, sailing through night and day—
    and to her soil: rich, rare, and sweet
        in our minds so be it.

Gratitude to Plants, the sun-facing light-changing leaf
    and fine root-hairs; standing still through wind
    and rain; their dance is in the flowing spiral grain
        in our minds so be it.

Gratitude to Air, bearing the soaring Swift and the silent
    Owl at dawn. Breath of our song
    clear spirit breeze
        in our minds so be it.

Gratitude to Wild Beings, our brothers and sisters, teaching
    secrets, freedoms, and ways; who share with us their
    milk; self-complete, brave, and aware
        in our minds so be it.

Gratitude to Water: clouds, lakes, rivers, glaciers;
    holding or releasing; streaming through all
    our bodies salty seas
        in our minds so be it.

Gratitude to the Sun: blinding pulsing light through
    trunks of trees, through mists, warming caves where
    bears and snakes sleep—he who wakes us—
        in our minds so be it.

Gratitude to the Great Sky
    who holds billions of stars—and goes yet beyond that—
    beyond all powers, and thoughts
    and yet is within us—
    Grandfather Space.
    The Mind is his Wife.

       so be it.

                  after a Mohawk prayer

MANZANITA

Before dawn the coyotes
    weave medicine songs
    dream nets—spirit baskets—
    milky way music
        they cook young girls with
        to be woman;
    or the whirling dance of
    striped boys—

At moon-set the pines are gold-purple
Just before sunrise.

The dog hastens into the undergrowth
Comes back panting
Huge, on the small dry flowers.

A woodpecker
Drums and echoes
Across the still meadow

One man draws, and releases   an arrow
Humming, flat,
Missing a gray stump, and splitting
A smooth red twisty manzanita bough.

Manzanita   the tips in fruit,
Clusters of hard green berries
The longer you look
The bigger they seem,

      "little apples"

Magpie's
Song

THE REAL WORK

*[Today with Zach & Dan rowing by Alcatraz
and around Angel Island]*

sea-lions and birds,
sun through fog
flaps up and lolling,
looks you dead in the eye.
sun haze;
a long tanker riding light and high.

sharp wave choppy line—
interface tide-flows—
seagulls sit on the meeting
eating;
we slide by white-stained cliffs.

the real work.
washing and sighing,
sliding by.

PINE TREE TOPS

in the blue night
frost haze, the sky glows
with the moon
pine tree tops
bend snow-blue, fade
into sky, frost, starlight.
the creak of boots.
rabbit tracks, deer tracks,
what do we know.

FOR NOTHING

Earth a flower
A phlox on the steep
slopes of light
hanging over the vast
solid spaces
small rotten crystals;
salts.

Earth a flower
by a gulf where a raven
flaps by once
a glimmer, a color
forgotten as all
falls away.

A flower
for nothing;
an offer;
no taker;

Snow-trickle, feldspar, dirt.

NIGHT HERONS

Night herons nest in the cypress
by the San Francisco
stationary boilers
with the high smoke stack
at the edge of the waters:
a steam turbine pump
to drive salt water
into the city's veins
mains
if the earth ever
quakes. and the power fails.
and water
to fight fire, runs
loose on the streets
with no pressure.

At the wire gate tilted slightly out
the part-wolf dog
would go in, to follow
if his human buddy lay on his side
and squirmed up first.

An abandoned, decaying, army.
a rotten rusty island prison
surrounded by lights of whirling
fluttering god-like birds
who truth
has never forgot.

I walk with my wife's sister
past the frozen bait;
with a long-bearded architect,
my dear brother,
and silent friend, whose

mustache curves wetly into his mouth
and he sometimes bites it.

the dog knows no laws and is strictly,
illegal. His neck arches and ears prick out
to catch mice in the tundra.
a black high school boy
drinking coffee at a fake green stand
tries to be friends with the dog,
and it works.

How could the
night herons ever come back?
to this noisy place on the bay.
like me.
the joy of all the beings
is in being
older and tougher and eaten
up.
in the tubes and lanes of things
in the sewers of bliss and judgment,
in the glorious cleansing
treatment
plants.

We pick our way
through the edge of the city
early
subtly spreading changing sky;

ever-fresh and lovely dawn.

THE EGG

"A snake-like beauty in the living changes of syntax"
—*Robert Duncan*

Kai twists
rubs "bellybutton"
rubs skin, front and back
two legs kicking
anus a sensitive center
    the pull-together
    between there and the scrotum,
the center line,
with the out-flyers changing
—fins, legs, wings,
feathers or fur,
they swing and swim
but the snake center
fire pushes through:
    mouth to ass,
    root to
    burning, steady,
    single eye.

breeze in the brown grasses
high clouds deep
blue.   white.
blue.   moving
changing

my Mother's old
soft arm. walking
helping up the
path.

Kai's hand
in my fist

the neck bones,
a little thread,
a garland,
of consonants and vowels
from the third eye
through the body's flowers
a string of peaks,
a whirlpool
sucking to the root.

It all gathers,
humming,
in the egg.

BY FRAZIER CREEK FALLS

Standing up on lifted, folded rock
looking out and down—

The creek falls to a far valley.
hills beyond that
facing, half-forested, dry
—clear sky
strong wind in the
stiff glittering needle clusters
of the pine—their brown
round trunk bodies
straight, still;
rustling trembling limbs and twigs

listen.

This living flowing land
is all there is, forever

We *are* it
it sings through us—

We could live on this Earth
without clothes or tools!

IT PLEASES

Far above the dome
Of the capitol—
          It's true!
A large bird soars
Against white cloud,
Wings arced,
Sailing easy in this
humid Southern sun-blurred
          breeze—
          the dark-suited policeman
          watches tourist cars—

And the center,
The center of power is nothing!
Nothing here.
Old white stone domes,
Strangely quiet people,

Earth-sky-bird patterns
          idly interlacing

The world does what it pleases.

                    XI 73, Washington, D.C.

MOTHER EARTH: HER WHALES

An owl winks in the shadows
A lizard lifts on tiptoe, breathing hard
Young male sparrow stretches up his neck,
        big head, watching—

The grasses are working in the sun. Turn it green.
Turn it sweet. That we may eat.
Grow our meat.

Brazil says "sovereign use of Natural Resources"
Thirty thousand kinds of unknown plants.
The living actual people of the jungle
        sold and tortured—
And a robot in a suit who peddles a delusion called "Brazil"
        can speak for *them?*

      The whales turn and glisten, plunge
          and sound and rise again,
      Hanging over subtly darkening deeps
      Flowing like breathing planets
         in the sparkling whorls of
            living light—

And Japan quibbles for words on
        what kinds of whales they can kill?
A once-great Buddhist nation
        dribbles methyl mercury
        like gonorrhea
           in the sea.

Père David's Deer, the Elaphure,
Lived in the tule marshes of the Yellow River
Two thousand years ago—and lost its home to rice—
The forests of Lo-yang were logged and all the silt &
Sand flowed down, and gone, by 1200 AD—

Wild Geese hatched out in Siberia
           head south over basins of the Chiang, the Ho,
           what we call "China"
On flyways they have used a million years.
Ah China, where are the tigers, the wild boars,
        the monkeys,
           like the snows of yesteryear
Gone in a mist, a flash, and the dry hard ground
Is parking space for fifty thousand trucks.
IS man most precious of all things?
—then let us love him, and his brothers, all those
Fading living beings—

North America, Turtle Island, taken by invaders
        who wage war around the world.
May ants, may abalone, otters, wolves and elk
Rise! and pull away their giving
        from the robot nations.

Solidarity. The People.
Standing Tree People!
Flying Bird People!
Swimming Sea People!
Four-legged, two-legged, people!

How can the head-heavy power-hungry politic scientist
Government   two-world   Capitalist-Imperialist
Third-world   Communist   paper-shuffling male
    non-farmer   jet-set   bureaucrats
Speak for the green of the leaf? Speak for the soil?

(Ah Margaret Mead . . . do you sometimes dream of Samoa?)

The robots argue how to parcel out our Mother Earth
To last a little longer
        like vultures flapping
Belching, gurgling,
        near a dying Doe.

"In yonder field a slain knight lies—
We'll fly to him and eat his eyes
                with a down
      derry derry derry down down."

            An Owl winks in the shadow
            A lizard lifts on tiptoe
                    breathing hard
            The whales turn and glisten
                    plunge and
            Sound, and rise again
            Flowing like breathing planets

            In the sparkling whorls

            Of living light.

                    40072, Stockholm: Summer Solstice

ETHNOBOTANY

In June two oak fell,
rot in the roots

Chainsaw in September
in three days one tree
bucked and quartered in the shed

sour fresh inner oak-wood smell
the main trunk splits
"like opening a book" (J. Tecklin)

And slightly humping oak leaves
deer muzzle and kick it,
Boletus.
one sort, *Alice Eastwood*
pink, and poison;

Two yellow. *edulis*
"edible and choice."
only I got just so slightly sick—

Taste all, and hand the knowledge down.

STRAIGHT-CREEK—GREAT BURN

for Tom and Martha Burch

Lightly, in the April mountains—
        Straight Creek,
dry grass freed again of snow
& the chickadees are pecking
last fall's seeds
      fluffing tail in chilly wind,

Avalanche piled up cross the creek
      and chunked-froze solid—
water sluicing under; spills out
      rock lip pool, bends over,
      braided, white, foaming,
returns to trembling
      deep-dark hole.

Creek boulders show the flow-wear lines
      in shapes the same
      as running blood
      carves in the heart's main
        valve,

Early spring dry. Dry snow flurries;
      walk on crusty high snow slopes
—grand dead burn pine—
      chartreuse lichen as adornment
        (a dye for wool)
angled tumbled talus rock
of geosyncline warm sea bottom
yes, so long ago.
"Once on a time."

Far light on the Bitteroots;
      scrabble down willow slide

changing clouds above,
shapes on glowing sun-ball
writhing,   choosing
          reaching out against eternal
                              azure—

us resting on dry fern and
                  watching

Shining Heaven
change his feather garments
          overhead.

A whoosh of birds
swoops up and round
tilts back
almost always flying all apart
and yet hangs on!
together;

never a leader,
all of one swift

empty
dancing   mind.

They arc and loop & then
their flight is done.
they settle down.
end of poem.

TWO FAWNS THAT DIDN'T SEE
THE LIGHT THIS SPRING

A friend in a tipi in the
Northern Rockies went out
hunting white tail with a
.22 and creeped up on a few
day-bedded, sleeping, shot
what he thought was a buck.
"It was a doe, and she was
carrying a fawn."
He cured the meat without
salt; sliced it following the
grain.

A friend in the Northern Sierra
hit a doe with her car. It
walked out calmly in the lights,
"And when we butchered her
there was a fawn—about so long—
so tiny—but all formed and right.
It had spots. And the little
hooves were soft and white."

TWO IMMORTALS

Sitting on a bench by the Rogue River, Oregon, looking at a landform map. Two older gents approached and one, with baseball cap, began to sing: "California Here I Come"—he must have seen the license. Asked me if I'd ever heard of Texas Slim. Yes. And he said the song "If I Had the Wings of an Angel" was his, had been writ by him, "I was in the penitentiary." "Let me shake your hand! That's a good song" I said, and he showed me his hand: faint blue traces of tattoo on the back, on the bent fingers. "And if I hit you with this hand it's L-O-V-E. And if I hit you with this hand it's H-A-T-E."

His friend, in a red and black buffalo check jacket stuck his hand out, under my nose, missing the forefinger. "How'd I lose that!" "How?" "An axe!"

Texas Slim said "I'm just giving him a ride. Last year his wife died." The two ambled off, chuckling, as Kai and Gen came running back up from the banks of Rogue River, hands full of round river stones.

Looking at the map, it was the space inside the loop of the upper Columbia, eastern Washington plateau country. "Channelled Scablands."

WHY LOG TRUCK DRIVERS RISE
EARLIER THAN STUDENTS OF ZEN

In the high seat, before-dawn dark,
Polished hubs gleam
And the shiny diesel stack
Warms and flutters
Up the Tyler Road grade
To the logging on Poorman creek.
Thirty miles of dust.

There is no other life.

*practice of log truck driver
is perhaps more demanding
than the practice of Zen?*

"ONE SHOULD NOT TALK TO A SKILLED HUNTER ABOUT WHAT IS FORBIDDEN BY THE BUDDHA"

—Hsiang-yen

A gray fox, female, nine pounds three ounces.
39 5/8″ long with tail.
Peeling skin back (Kai
reminded us to chant the *Shingyo* first)
cold pelt. crinkle; and musky smell
mixed with dead-body odor starting.

Stomach content: a whole ground squirrel well chewed
plus one lizard foot
and somewhere from inside the ground squirrel
a bit of aluminum foil.

The secret.
and the secret hidden deep in that.

LMFBR

Death himself
     (Liquid Metal Fast Breeder Reactor)
     stands grinning, beckoning.
Plutonium tooth-glow.
Eyebrows buzzing.
Strip-mining scythe.

Kālī dances on the dead stiff cock.

     Aluminum beer cans, plastic spoons,
plywood veneer, PVC pipe, vinyl seat covers,
        don't exactly burn, don't quite rot,
        flood over us,

        robes and garbs
        of the Kālī-yūga

        end of days.

MAGPIE'S SONG

Six A.M.,
Sat down on excavation gravel
by juniper and desert S.P. tracks
interstate 80 not far off
    between trucks
Coyotes—maybe three
        howling and yapping from a rise.

Magpie on a bough
Tipped his head and said,

    "Here in the mind, brother
    Turquoise blue.
    I wouldn't fool you.
    Smell the breeze
    It came through all the trees
    No need to fear
    What's ahead
    Snow up on the hills west
    Will be there every year
    be at rest.
    A feather on the ground—
    The wind sound—

Here in the Mind, Brother,
Turquoise Blue"

For
The Children

GEN

Gen
little frown
buried in her breast
    and long black hair
Gen for milk
Gen for sleep
Gen for looking-over-shoulder
far beyond the waving eucalyptus
      limbs and farther dreaming crow
flying slow and steady for the ocean;
eyes over drippy nipple
    at the rising shadow sun
whales of cool and dark,
Gen patted-on-the-head by Kai,
"don't cry"

TOMORROW'S SONG

The USA slowly lost its mandate
in the middle and later twentieth century
it never gave the mountains and rivers,
      trees and animals,
         a vote.
all the people turned away from it
      myths die; even continents are impermanent

      Turtle Island returned.
      my friend broke open a dried coyote-scat
      removed a ground squirrel tooth
      pierced it, hung it
      from the gold ring
      in his ear.

We look to the future with pleasure
we need no fossil fuel
get power within
grow strong on less.

Grasp the tools and move in rhythm side by side
      flash gleams of wit and silent knowledge
         eye to eye
sit still like cats or snakes or stones
      as whole and holding as
         the blue black sky.
gentle and innocent as wolves
      as tricky as a prince.

At work and in our place:

      in the service
      of the wilderness
      of life
      of death
      of the Mother's breasts!

WHAT HAPPENED HERE BEFORE

—300,000,000—

First a sea: soft sands, muds, and marls
        —loading, compressing, heating, crumpling,
            crushing, recrystallizing, infiltrating,
several times lifted and submerged.
intruding molten granite magma
        deep-cooled and speckling,
            gold quartz fills the cracks—

—80,000,000—

sea-bed strata raised and folded,
        granite far below.
warm quiet centuries of rains
        (make dark red tropic soils)
            wear down two miles of surface,
lay bare the veins and tumble heavy gold
        in streambeds
                slate and schist rock-riffles catch it—
volcanic ash floats down and dams the streams,
        piles up the gold and gravel—

—3,000,000—

flowing north, two rivers joined,
        to make a wide long lake.
and then it tilted and the rivers fell apart
        all running west
            to cut the gorges of the Feather,
                Bear, and Yuba.

Ponderosa pine, manzanita, black oak, mountain yew.
        deer, coyote, bluejay, gray squirrel,
            ground squirrel, fox, blacktail hare,

251

                    ringtail, bobcat, bear,
                            all came to live here.

                            —40,000—

    And human people came with basket hats and nets
                    winter-houses underground
                    yew bows painted green,
                        feasts and dances for the boys and girls
                            songs and stories in the smoky dark.

                            —150—

    Then came the white man: tossed up trees and
                        boulders with big hoses,
                            going after that old gravel and the gold.
    horses, apple-orchards, card-games,
                        pistol-shooting, churches, county jail.

                            ➾

    We asked, who the land belonged to.
                    and where one pays tax.
    (two gents who never used it twenty years,
    and before them the widow
                    of the son of the man
                    who got him a patented deed
                    on a worked-out mining claim,)
    laid hasty on land that was deer and acorn
                    grounds of the Nisenan?
                    branch of the Maidu?

    (they never had a chance to speak, even,
                    their name.)
    (and who remembers the Treaty of Guadalupe Hidalgo.)

                    the land belongs to itself.
                    "no self in self; no self in things"

Turtle Island swims
in the ocean-sky swirl-void
biting its tail while the worlds go
            on-and-off
                winking

& Mr. Tobiassen, a Cousin Jack,
            assesses the county tax.
(the tax is our body-mind, guest at the banquet
            Memorial and Annual, in honor
            of sunlight grown heavy and tasty
            while moving up food-chains
in search of a body with eyes and a fairly large
                brain—
            to look back at itself
                on high.)

                    now,

we sit here near the diggings
in the forest, by our fire, and watch
the moon and planets and the shooting stars—

my sons ask, who are we?
drying apples picked from homestead trees
drying berries, curing meat,
shooting arrows at a bale of straw.

military jets head northeast, roaring, every dawn.
my sons ask, who are they?

            *WE SHALL SEE
            WHO KNOWS
            HOW TO BE*

Bluejay screeches from a pine.

TOWARD CLIMAX

I.

salt seas, mountains, deserts—
cell mandala holding water
nerve network linking toes and eyes
fins   legs   wings—
teeth, all-purpose little early mammal molars.
primate flat-foot
front fore-mounted eyes—

watching at the forest-grassland (interface
richness) edge.
scavenge, gather, rise up on rear legs.
running—grasping—hand and eye;
hunting.
calling others to the stalk, the drive.

note sharp points of split bone; broken rock.

brain-size blossoming
on the balance of the neck,
tough skin—good eyes—sharp ears—
move in bands.
milkweed fiber rolled out on the thigh;
        nets to carry fruits or meat.

catch fire, move on.
eurasia tundra reindeer herds
sewn hide clothing, mammoth-rib-framework tent.

Bison, bear,   skinned and split;
    opening animal chests and bellies, skulls,
    bodies just like ours—
pictures in caves.

send sound off the mouth and lips
formal complex grammars transect
    inner structures & the daily world—

big herds dwindle
    (—did we kill them?
    thousand-mile front of prairie fire—)
ice age warms up
learn more plants. netting, trapping, boats.
bow and arrow. dogs.
mingle bands and families in and out like language
    kin to grubs and trees and wolves

    dance and sing.
begin to go "beyond"—   reed flute—
    buried baby wrapped in many furs—
great dream-time tales to tell.

squash blossom in the garbage heap.
    start farming.
cows won't stay away, start herding.
weaving, throwing clay.
get better off, get class,
make lists, start writing down.

    forget wild plants, their virtues
    lose dream-time
    lose largest size of brain—

get safer, tighter, wrapped in,
winding smaller, spreading wider,
lay towns out in streets in rows,
and build a wall.

drain swamp for wet-rice grasses, burn back woods,
herd men like cows.
have slaves build a fleet

raid for wealth—bronze weapons
horse and wagon—iron—war.

study stars and figure central
never-moving Pole Star King.

❦

II.

From "King" project a Law. (Foxy self-survival sense is Reason,
since it "works") and Reason gets ferocious as it goes for order
throughout nature—turns Law back on nature. (A rooster was
burned at the stake for laying an egg. Unnatural. 1474.)

❦

III.

science walks in beauty:

nets are many knots
skin is border-guard, a pelt is borrowed warmth;
a bow is the flex of a limb in the wind
a giant downtown building
        is a creekbed stood on end.

detritus pathways. "delayed and complex ways
to pass the food through webs."

maturity. stop and think. draw on the mind's
stored richness. memory, dream, half-digested

image of your life. "detritus pathways"—feed
the many tiny things that feed an owl.
send heart boldly travelling,
on the heat of the dead & down.

IV.

TWO LOGGING SONGS

CLEAR-CUT

Forestry. "How
Many people
Were harvested
In Viet-Nam?"

Clear-cut. "Some
Were children,
Some were over-ripe."

VIRGIN

A virgin
Forest
Is ancient; many-
Breasted,
Stable; at
Climax.

WITHOUT

the silence
of nature
within.

the power within.
the power

without.

the path is whatever passes—no
end in itself.

the end is,
grace—ease—

healing,
not saving.

singing
the proof

the proof of the power within.

FOR THE CHILDREN

The rising hills, the slopes,
of statistics
lie before us.
the steep climb
of everything, going up,
up, as we all
go down.

In the next century
or the one beyond that,
they say,
are valleys, pastures,
we can meet there in peace
if we make it.

To climb these coming crests
one word to you, to
you and your children:

stay together
learn the flowers
go light

AS FOR POETS

As for poets
The Earth Poets
Who write small poems,
Need help from no man.

The Air Poets
Play out the swiftest gales
And sometimes loll in the eddies.
Poem after poem,
Curling back on the same thrust.

At fifty below
Fuel oil won't flow
And propane stays in the tank.
Fire Poets
Burn at absolute zero
Fossil love pumped back up.

The first
Water Poet
Stayed down six years.
He was covered with seaweed.
The life in his poem
Left millions of tiny
Different tracks
Criss-crossing through the mud.

With the Sun and Moon
In his belly,
The Space Poet
Sleeps.
No end to the sky—
But his poems,
Like wild geese,
Fly off the edge.

A Mind Poet
Stays in the house.
The house is empty
And it has no walls.
The poem
Is seen from all sides,
Everywhere,
At once.

伐柯如何
匪斧不克
取妻如何
匪媒不得

伐柯伐柯
其則不遠
我覯之子
籩豆有踐

from

Axe
Handles

How do you shape an axe handle?
Without an axe it can't be done.
How do you take a wife?
Without a go-between you can't get one.
Shape a handle, shape a handle,
the pattern is not far off.
And here's a girl I know,
The wine and food in rows.

From *Book of Songs (Shih Ching)*
(Mao no. 158): A folk song from
the Pin area, 5th c. B.C.

FOR/FROM LEW

Lew Welch just turned up one day,
live as you and me. "Damn, Lew" I said,
"you didn't shoot yourself after all."
"Yes I did" he said,
and even then I felt the tingling down my back.
"Yes you did, too" I said—"I can feel it now."
"Yeah" he said,
"There's a basic fear between your world and
mine. I don't know why.
What I came to say was,
teach the children about the cycles.
The life cycles. All the other cycles.
That's what it's all about, and it's all forgot."

Loops

AXE HANDLES

One afternoon the last week in April
Showing Kai how to throw a hatchet
One-half turn and it sticks in a stump.
He recalls the hatchet-head
Without a handle, in the shop
And go gets it, and wants it for his own.
A broken-off axe handle behind the door
Is long enough for a hatchet,
We cut it to length and take it
With the hatchet head
And working hatchet, to the wood block.
There I begin to shape the old handle
With the hatchet, and the phrase
First learned from Ezra Pound
Rings in my ears!
"When making an axe handle
        the pattern is not far off."
And I say this to Kai
"Look: We'll shape the handle
By checking the handle
Of the axe we cut with—"
And he sees. And I hear it again:
It's in Lu Ji's *Wên Fu,* fourth century
A.D. "Essay on Literature"—in the
Preface: "In making the handle
Of an axe
By cutting wood with an axe
The model is indeed near at hand."
My teacher Shih-hsiang Chen
Translated that and taught it years ago
And I see: Pound was an axe,
Chen was an axe, I am an axe
And my son a handle, soon
To be shaping again, model
And tool, craft of culture,
How we go on.

RIVER IN THE VALLEY

We cross the Sacramento River at Colusa
follow the road on the levee south and east
find thousands of swallows nesting
on the underside of a concrete overhead
roadway? causeway? abandoned. Near
                 Butte Creek.

     Gen runs in little circles looking up
     at swoops of swallows—laughing—
               they keep
     flowing under the bridge and out,

     Kai leans silent against a concrete pier
     tries to hold with his eyes the course
     of a single darting bird,

     I pick grass seeds from my socks.

The coast range. Parched yellow front hills,
blue-gray thornbrush higher hills behind.
And here is the Great Central Valley,
drained, then planted and watered,
     thousand-foot deep soils
     thousand-acre orchards

     Sunday morning,
only one place serving breakfast
in Colusa, old river and tractor men
sipping milky coffee.

From north of Sutter Buttes
we see snow on Mt. Lassen
and the clear arc of the Sierra
south to the Desolation peaks.
One boy asks, "where do rivers start?"

in threads in hills, and gather down to here—
but the river
is all of it everywhere,
all flowing at once,
all one place.

BERRY TERRITORY

*Walking the woods on an early spring dry day, the slopes behind Lanes
Landing Farm on the Kentucky River, with Tanya and Wendell*

Under dead leaves Tanya finds a tortoise
    matching the leaves—legs pulled in—

And we look at woodchuck holes that dive
    under limestone ledges
    seabottom strata,
    who lives there brushes furry back
    on shell and coral,

Most holes with leaves and twigs around the door,
    nobody in.

Wendell, crouched down,
    sticks his face in a woodchuck hole
    "Hey, smell that, it's a fox!"
    I go on my knees,
    put the opening to my face
    like a mask. No light;
    all smell: sour—warm—
    Splintered bones, scats? feathers?
    Wreathing bodies—wild—

Some home.

THE COOL AROUND THE FIRE

Drink black coffee from a thermos
      sitting on a stump.

       piles burn down, the green limb
       fringe edge
       picked up and tossed in
To the center: white ash mound
      shimmering red within.
      tip head down
      to shield face
      with hat brim   from the heat;

The thinning, pruning, brush-cut
      robbed from bugs and fungus—
      belly gray clouds
      swing low soft over
      maybe rain, bring an end
      to this drouth;

Burn brush to take heat
      from next summer's wildfires
      and to bring rain on time,
      and fires clear the tangle.

      the tangle of the heart.
Black coffee, bitter, hot,
      smoke rises straight and calm
      air
Still and cool.

CHANGING DIAPERS

How intelligent he looks!
    on his back
    both feet caught in my one hand
    his glance set sideways,
    on a giant poster of Geronimo
    with a Sharp's repeating rifle by his knee.

I open, wipe, he doesn't even notice
    nor do I.
Baby legs and knees
    toes like little peas
    little wrinkles, good-to-eat,
    eyes bright, shiny ears,
    chest swelling drawing air,

No trouble, friend,
    you and me   and Geronimo
    are men.

PAINTING THE NORTH SAN JUAN SCHOOL

White paint splotches on blue head bandanas
Dusty transistor with wired-on antenna
    plays sixties rock and roll;
Little kids came with us are on teeter-totters
    tilting under shade of oak
This building good for ten years more.
The shingled bell-cupola trembles
    at every log truck rolling by—

The radio speaks:
    today it will be one hundred degrees in the valley.
—Franquette walnuts grafted on the
    local native rootstock do o.k.
    nursery stock of cherry all has fungus;
Lucky if a bare-root planting lives,

This paint thins with water.
This year the busses will run only
    on paved roads,
Somehow the children will be taught:
How to record their mother tongue
    with written signs,

Names to call the landscape of the continent
                they live on
Assigned it by the ruling people of the last
    three hundred years,
The games of numbers,
What went before, as told by those who
    think they know it,

A drunken man with chestnut mustache
Stumbles off the road to ask if he can help.

Children drinking chocolate milk

Ladders resting on the shaky porch.

FENCE POSTS

It might be that horses would be useful
On a snowy morning to take the trail
Down the ridge to visit Steve or Mike and
Faster than going around the gravelled road by car.

So the thought came to fence a part of the forest,
Thin trees and clear the brush,
Ron splits cedar rails and fenceposts
On Black Sands Placer road where he gets
These great old butt logs from the Camptonville sawmill
Why they can't use them I don't know—
They aren't all pecky.
He delivers, too, in a bread van
His grandfather drove in Seattle.

Sapwood posts are a little bit cheaper than heartwood.
I could have bought all heartwood from the start
But then I thought how it doesn't work
To always make a point of getting the best which is why
I sometimes pick out the worse and damaged looking fruit
And vegetables at the market because I know
I actually will enjoy them in any case but
Some people might take them as second choice
And feel sour about it all evening.

With sapwood fenceposts
You ought to soak to make sure they won't rot
In a fifty-five gallon drum with penta 10 to 1
Which is ten gallons of oil and a gallon of
Termite and fungus poison.
I use old crankcase oil to dilute
And that's a good thing to do with it but,
There's not really enough old crank to go around.
The posts should be two feet in the ground.

So, soaking six posts a week at a time
The soaked pile getting bigger week by week,
But the oil only comes up one and a half feet.
I could add kerosene in
At seventy cents a gallon
Which is what it costs when you buy it by the drum
And that's $3.50 to raise the soaking level up
Plus a half a can of penta more, six dollars,
For a hundred and twenty fence posts
On which I saved thirty dollars by getting the sapwood,
But still you have to count your time,

A well-done fence is beautiful.
And horses, too.
Penny wise pound foolish either way.

Spring 77

LOOK BACK

Twice one summer
I walked up Piute mountain,
our trailcrew was camped at Bear Valley.
I first had chainsaw practice
cutting wood there for the cook.
Piute mountain. And scanned the crest
of the Sawtooths, to the east.
A Whitebark pine relict stand
cut off from friends
by miles of air and granite—me
running out ridges.
Jimmy Jones the cook said "I
used to do that, run the ridges
all day long—just like a coyote."
When I built a little sweatlodge
one Sunday by the creek
he told me to be careful,
and almost came in too.

Today at Slide Peak in the Sawtooths
I look back at that mountain
twenty-five years. Those days
when I lived and thought all alone.

I was studying Chinese
preparing for Asia
every night after trail crew work
                              from a book.
Jimmy Jones was a Mariposa Indian.
One night by the campfire
drinking that coffee black
he stood there looking down at my
H.G. Creel, "Those letters Chinese?"
"Yes," I said. He said, "Hmmmmm.
My grandpa they say was Chinese."

And that year I quit early.
told the foreman I was headed for Japan.
He looked like he knew, and said "Bechtel."
I couldn't tell him something strange as Zen.

Jimmy Jones, and these mountains and creeks.
The up and down of it
stays in my feet.

VII 78, The Sawtooths

SOY SAUCE

for Bruce Boyd and Holly Tornheim

Standing on a stepladder
       up under hot ceiling
tacking on wire net for plaster,
a day's work helping Bruce and Holly on their house,
I catch a sour salt smell and come back
       down the ladder.

"Deer lick it nights" she says,
and shows me the frame of the window she's planing,
clear redwood, but dark, with a smell.

"Scored a broken-up, two-thousand-gallon redwood
soy sauce tank from a company went out of business
down near San Jose."

Out in the yard the staves are stacked:
I lean over, sniff them, ah! it's like Shinshu miso,
the darker saltier miso paste of the Nagano
uplands, central main island, Japan—
it's like Shinshu pickles!

I see in mind my friend Shimizu Yasushi and me,
one October years ago, trudging through days of snow
crossing the Japan Alps and descending
the last night, to a farmhouse,
taking a late hot bath in the dark—and eating
       a bowl of chill miso radish pickles,
       nothing ever so good!

Back here, hot summer sunshine dusty yard,
       hammer in hand.

But I know how it tastes
    to lick those window frames
    in the dark,
        the deer.

STRATEGIC AIR COMMAND

The hiss and flashing lights of a jet
Pass near Jupiter in Virgo.
He asks, how many satellites in the sky?
Does anyone know where they all are?
What are they doing, who watches them?

Frost settles on the sleeping bags.
The last embers of fire,
One more cup of tea,
At the edge of a high lake rimmed with snow.

These cliffs and the stars
Belong to the same universe.
This little air in between
Belongs to the twentieth century and its wars.

VIII 82, Koip Peak, Sierra Nevada

WORKING ON THE '58 WILLYS PICKUP
For Lu Yu

The year this truck was made
I sat in early morning darkness
Chanting sūtra in Kyoto,
And spent the days studying Chinese.
Chinese, Japanese, Sanskrit, French—
Joys of Dharma-scholarship
And the splendid old temples—
But learned nothing of trucks.

Now to bring sawdust
Rotten and rich
From a sawmill abandoned when I was just born
Lost in the young fir and cedar
At Bloody Run Creek
So that clay in the garden
Can be broken and tempered
And growing plants mulched to save water—
And to also haul gravel
From the old placer diggings,
To screen it and mix in the sand with the clay
Putting pebbles aside to strew on the paths
So muddy in winter—

I lie in the dusty and broken bush
Under the pickup
Already thought to be old—
Admiring its solidness, square lines,
Thinking a truck like this
would please Chairman Mao.

The rear end rebuilt and put back
With new spider gears,

Brake cylinders cleaned, the brake drums
New-turned and new brake shoes,
Taught how to do this
By friends who themselves spent
Youth with the Classics—

The garden gets better, I
Laugh in the evening
To pick up Chinese
And read about farming,
I fix truck and lock eyebrows
With tough-handed men of the past.

GETTING IN THE WOOD

The sour smell,
   blue stain,
      water squirts out round the wedge,

Lifting quarters of rounds
   covered with ants,
  "a living glove of ants upon my hand"
the poll of the sledge a bit peened over
so the wedge springs off and tumbles
   ringing like high-pitched bells
      into the complex duff of twigs
      poison oak, bark, sawdust,
      shards of logs,

And the sweat drips down.
   Smell of crushed ants.
The lean and heave on the peavey
that breaks free the last of a bucked
   three-foot round,
      it lies flat on smashed oaklings—

Wedge and sledge, peavey and maul,
   little axe, canteen, piggyback can
   of saw-mix gas and oil for the chain,
knapsack of files and goggles and rags,

All to gather the dead and the down.
   the young men throw splits on the piles
   bodies hardening, learning the pace
and the smell of tools from this delve
   in the winter
      death-topple of elderly oak.
Four cords.

TRUE NIGHT

Sheath of sleep in the black of the bed:
From outside this dream womb
Comes a clatter
Comes a clatter
And finally the mind rises up to a fact
Like a fish to a hook
A raccoon at the kitchen!
A falling of metal bowls,
    the clashing of jars,
    the avalanche of plates!
I snap alive to this ritual
Rise unsteady, find my feet,
Grab the stick, dash in the dark—
I'm a huge pounding demon
That roars at raccoons—
They whip round the corner,
A scratching sound tells me
    they've gone up a tree.

I stand at the base
Two young ones that perch on
Two dead stub limbs and
Peer down from both sides of the trunk:
    Roar, roar, I roar
    you awful raccoons, you wake me
    up nights, you ravage
    our kitchen

As I stay there then silent
The chill of the air on my nakedness
Starts off the skin
I am all alive to the night.
Bare foot shaping on gravel
Stick in the hand, forever.

Long streak of cloud giving way
To a milky thin light
Back of black pine bough,
The moon is still full,
Hillsides of Pine trees all
Whispering; crickets still cricketting
Faint in cold coves in the dark

I turn and walk slow
Back the path to the beds
With goosebumps and loose waving hair
In the night of milk-moonlit thin cloud glow
And black rustling pines
I feel like a dandelion head
Gone to seed
About to be blown all away
Or a sea anemone open and waving in
cool pearly water.

Fifty years old.
I still spend my time
Screwing nuts down on bolts.

At the shadow pool,
Children are sleeping,
And a lover I've lived with for years,
True night.
One cannot stay too long awake
In this dark

Dusty feet, hair tangling,
I stoop and slip back to the
Sheath, for the sleep I still need,
For the waking that comes
Every day

With the dawn.

Little Songs
for Gaia

across salt marshes north of
San Francisco Bay
cloud soft grays
blues little fuzzies
illusion structures—pale blue of the edge,
    sky behind,

hawk dipping and circling
over salt marsh

ah, this slow-paced
system of systems, whirling and turning

a five-thousand-year span
    about all that a human can figure,

grasshopper man in his car driving through.

✺

The manzanita succession story—

Shady lady,
    makes the boys
        turn gray.

✺

        trout-of-the-air, ouzel,
      bouncing, dipping, on a round rock
   round as the hump of snow-on-grass beside it
    between the icy banks, the running stream:
        and into running stream

right in!

you   fly

❧

As the crickets' soft autumn hum
is to us,
so are we to the trees

as are they

to the rocks and the hills.

❧

Awakened by the clock striking five
Already light,
I still see the dream
Three Corn Maidens in green
Green leaves, skirt, sleeves—
Walking by.
    I turned my eyes, knowing not to stare.

And wake thinking
I should have looked more
To see the way they were
Corn Maidens in green.
Green leaf face, too
Eyes turned aside.

But then I'm glad for once I knew
Not to look too much when
Really there.

    Or try to write it down.

＊

Red-shafted
Flicker—
      sharp cool call

The smell of Sweet Birch blooms
Through the warm manzanita

And the soft raining-down
Invisible, crackling dry duff,

      of the droppings of oak-moth caterpillars.
      nibbling spring leaves

High in the oak limbs above.

＊

      Hear bucks skirmishing in the night—

         the light, playful rattle
      ·   of antlers
       in a circle of moonlight
    between the pond and the barn,
     and the dancing-pushing-
    stamping—and off running,
     open the door to go out
    to the chickencoop for eggs

＊

Log trucks go by at four in the morning
        as we roll in our sleeping bags
                dreaming of health.
The log trucks remind us,
        as we think, dream and play

of the world that is carried away.

❧

Steep cliff ledge, a pair of young raptors
        their hawklet-hood hanging
        over blue lake   over space

The flat green hayfields
        gleaming white *playa*   below

Hawks, eagles, and swallows
        nesting in holes between
                        layers of rock

Life of,
        sailing out over worlds up and down.
        blue mountain desert,
        cliff by a blue-green lake.

                                The Warner Range

❧

Dead doe lying in the rain

    on the shoulder
    in the gravel

I see your stiff leg

    in the headlights
    by the roadside

Dead doe lying in the rain

❧

THE FLICKERS

sharp clear call

THIS!

THIS!

THIS!

in the cool pine breeze

❧

Hers was not a
Sheath.
It was
A
Quiver.

I am sorry I disturbed you.

I broke into your house last night
To use the library.
There were some things I had to look up;
A large book fell
          and knocked over others.
Afraid you'd wake and find me
and be truly alarmed
                    I left
Without picking up.

I got your name from the mailbox
As I fled, to write you and explain.

Nets

THREE DEER ONE COYOTE RUNNING
IN THE SNOW

First three deer bounding
and then coyote streaks right after
        tail   *flat out*

I stand dumb a while   two seconds
blankly black-and-white of trees and snow

        Coyote's back!
        good coat, fluffy tail,
sees me: quickly gone.

        Later:
I walk through where they ran

to study how that news all got put down.

24:IV:40075, 3:30 PM,
N. OF COALDALE, NEVADA, A GLIMPSE THROUGH
A BREAK IN THE STORM OF THE SUMMIT OF THE
WHITE MOUNTAINS

O Mother Gaia

sky   cloud   gate   milk   snow

wind-void-word

I bow in roadside gravel

TALKING LATE WITH THE GOVERNOR
ABOUT THE BUDGET

for Jerry Brown

Entering the midnight
Halls of the capitol,
Iron carts full of printed bills
Filling life with rules,

At the end of many chambers
Alone in a large tan room
The Governor sits, without dinner.
Scanning the hills of laws—budgets—codes—
In this land of twenty million
From desert to ocean.

Till the oil runs out
There's no end in sight.
Outside, his car waits with driver
Alone, engine idling.
The great pines on the Capitol grounds
Are less than a century old.

Two A.M.,
We walk to the street
Tired of the effort
Of thinking about "the People."
The half-moon travels west
In the elegant company
Of Jupiter and Aldebaran,

And east, over the Sierra,
Far flashes of lightning—
Is it raining tonight at home?

"HE SHOT ARROWS, BUT NOT
AT BIRDS PERCHING"

Lun yü, VII, 26

The Governor came to visit in the mountains
    we cleaned the house and raked the yard that day.
He'd been east and hadn't slept much
    so napped all afternoon back in the shade.

Young trees and chickens must be tended
    I sprayed apples, and took water to the hens.
Next day we read the papers, spoke of farming,
    of oil, and what would happen to the cars.

And then beside the pond we started laughing,
    got the quiver and bow and strung the bow.
Arrow after arrow flashing
    hissing under pines in summer breeze

Striking deep in straw bales by the barn.

Summer 76

WHAT HAVE I LEARNED

What have I learned but
the proper use for several tools?

The moments
between hard pleasant tasks

To sit silent, drink wine,
and think my own kind
of dry crusty thoughts.

    —the first Calochortus flowers
    and in all the land,
        it's spring.
    I point them out:
    the yellow petals, the golden hairs,
        to Gen.

Seeing in silence:
never the same twice,
but when you get it right,

    you pass it on.

DILLINGHAM, ALASKA, THE WILLOW TREE BAR

Drills chatter full of mud and compressed air
all across the globe,
    low-ceilinged bars, we hear the same new songs

All the new songs.
In the working bars of the world.
After you done drive Cat. After the truck
        went home.
        Caribou slip,
        front legs folded first
        under the warm oil pipeline
        set four feet off the ground—

On the wood floor, glass in hand,
        laugh and cuss with
        somebody else's wife.
        Texans, Hawaiians, Eskimos,
        Filipinos, Workers, always
        on the edge of a brawl—
        In the bars of the world.
        Hearing those same new songs
                in Abadan,
        Naples, Galveston, Darwin, Fairbanks,
        White or brown,
Drinking it down,

the pain
of the work
of wrecking the world.

REMOVING THE PLATE OF THE PUMP
ON THE HYDRAULIC SYSTEM OF THE BACKHOE

for Burt Hybart

Through mud, fouled nuts, black grime
it opens, a gleam of spotless steel
machined-fit perfect
swirl of intake and output
relentless clarity
at the heart
of work.

ULURU WILD FIG SONG

1

Soft earth turns straight up
curls out and away from its base
hard and red—a dome—five miles around
                Ayers Rock, Uluru,

we push through grasses, vines, bushes
along the damp earth wash-off watershed margin
    where vertical rock dives
        into level sand,

Clustering chittering zebra finches on the
            bone-white twigs,
red-eyed pink-foot little dove,

push on, into caves of overhangs,
painted red circles in circles,
black splayed-out human bodies,
painted lizards, wavy lines.

skip across sandy peels of clean bent bedrock
stop for lunch and there's a native fig tree
heavy-clustered, many ripe:
someone must have sat here, shat here
              long ago.

2

Sit in the dust
    take the clothes off. feel it on the skin
    lay down. roll around
    run sand through your hair.
    nap an hour

bird calls through dreams
                now
            you're clean.

sitting on red sand ground with a dog.
breeze blowing, full moon,
women singing over there—
men clapping sticks and singing here

                eating meaty bone,
                hold the dog off with one foot

            stickers & prickles in the sand—

clacking the boomerang beat,
            a long walk
        singing the land.

3
                naked but decorated,
                    scarred.
                white ash   white clay,
                    scars on the chest.
lines of scars on the loin.
the scars: the gate,
                the path, the seal,
                    the proof.

white-barred birds under the dark sky.

4
        singing and drumming at the school
a blonde-haired black-skinned girl
            watching and same time teasing a friend
dress half untied, naked beneath,

young breasts like the *mulpu*
                    mushroom,
swelling up through sand.

                    stiff wind close to the ground,
                    trash lodged in the spinifex, the fence,
                    the bottles, broken cars.

5
Sit down in the sand
                    skin to the ground.
                    a thousand miles of open gritty land

                    white cockatoo on a salt pan

hard wild fig on the tongue.

                    this wild fig song.

                         Fall of 40081, Uluru, Amata, Fregon,
                              Papunya, Ilpili, Austral.

OLD ROTTING TREE TRUNK DOWN

Winding grain
Of twisting outer spiral shell

Stubby broken limbs at angles
Peeled off outer layers askew;
A big rock
Locked in taproot clasp
Now lifted to the air;
Amber beads of ancient sap
In powdery cracks of red dry-rot
                fallen away
From the pitchy heartwood core.

Beautiful body we walk on:
Up and across to miss
                the wiry manzanita mat.
On a slope of rock and air,
Of breeze without cease—

     If "meditation on decay and rot cures lust"
     I'm hopeless:
     I delight in thought of fungus,
     beetle larvae, stains
             that suck the life still
             from your old insides,

Under crystal sky.
And the woodpecker flash
     from tree to tree
     in a grove of your heirs
On the green-watered bench right there!

     Looking out at blue lakes,
     dripping snowpatch

soaking glacial rubble,
crumbling rocky cliffs and scree,

Corruption, decay, the sticky turnover—
Death into more of the
Life-death same,

A quick life:
and the long slow
feeding that follows—
the woodpecker's cry.

VII 78, English Mountain

OLD WOMAN NATURE

Old Woman Nature
naturally has a bag of bones
      tucked away somewhere.
      a whole room full of bones!

A scattering of hair and cartilage
    bits in the woods.

A fox scat with hair and a tooth in it.
    a shellmound
        a bone flake in a streambank.

A purring cat, crunching
    the mouse head first,
        eating on down toward the tail—

The sweet old woman
    calmly gathering firewood in the
            moon . . .

Don't be shocked,
She's heating you some soup.

               VII 81, Seeing Ichikawa Ennosuke in
      "Kurozuka"—"Demoness"—at the Kabuki-za in Tokyo

THE CANYON WREN

for James and Carol Katz

I look up at the cliffs
But we're swept on by   downriver
                                                  the rafts
Wobble and slide over roils of water
        boulders shimmer
        under the arching stream
Rock walls straight up on both sides.
A hawk cuts across that narrow sky
                                        hit by sun,

We paddle forward, backstroke, turn,
Spinning through eddies and waves
Stairsteps of churning whitewater.
        above the roar
        hear the song of a Canyon Wren.

A smooth stretch, drifting and resting.
Hear it again, delicate downward song

        ti ti   ti ti tee tee tee

Descending through ancient beds.
A single female mallard flies upstream—

Shooting the Hundred-Pace Rapids
Su Shih saw, for a moment,
        it all stand still
"I stare at the water:
        it moves with unspeakable slowness"

Dōgen, writing at midnight,

"mountains flow

"water is the palace of the dragon
"it does not flow away.

We beach up at China Camp
Between piles of stone
Stacked there by black-haired miners,
      cook in the dark
        sleep all night long by the stream.

These songs that are here and gone,
Here and gone,
To purify our ears.

The Stanislaus River runs through Central Miwok country and down
to the San Joaquin valley. The twists and turns of the river, the
layering, swirling stone cliffs of the gorges are cut in nine-million-
year-old latites. For many seasons lovers of rocks and water have
danced in rafts and kayaks down this dragon-arm of the high Sierra.
Not long ago Jim Katz and friends, river runners all, asked me to
shoot the river with them, to see its face once more before it goes
under the rising waters of the New Mellones Dam. The song of the
Canyon Wren stayed with us the whole voyage; at China Camp, in
the dark, I wrote this poem.

April 40081, Stanislaus River, Camp 9 to
Parrott's Ferry

FOR ALL

Ah to be alive
      on a mid-September morn
      fording a stream
      barefoot, pants rolled up,
      holding boots, pack on,
      sunshine, ice in the shallows,
      northern rockies.

Rustle and shimmer of icy creek waters
stones turn underfoot, small and hard as toes
      cold nose dripping
      singing inside
      creek music, heart music,
      smell of sun on gravel.

      I pledge allegiance

I pledge allegiance to the soil
      of Turtle Island,
and to the beings who thereon dwell
      one ecosystem
      in diversity
      under the sun
With joyful interpenetration for all.

from

Left Out
in the Rain

❦ *For Donald Allen and James Laughlin*

A MISCELLANY

This section is in part a gathering of poems
uncollected in earlier books. It contains some
very early poems as well as a number of
formalistic, epigrammatic, and experimental
poems.

ELK TRAILS

Ancient, world-old Elk paths
Narrow, dusty Elk paths
Wide-trampled, muddy,
Aimless . . . wandering . . .
Everchanging Elk paths.

I have walked you, ancient trails,
Along the narrow rocky ridges
High above the mountains that
Make up your world:
Looking down on giant trees, silent
In the purple shadows of ravines—
Above the spire-like alpine fir
Above the high, steep-slanting meadows
Where sun-softened snowfields share the earth
With flowers.

I have followed narrow twisting ridges,
Sharp-topped and jagged as a broken crosscut saw
Across the roof of all the Elk-world
On one ancient wandering trail,
Cutting crazily over rocks and dust and snow—
Gently slanting through high meadows,
Rich with scent of Lupine,
Rich with smell of Elk-dung,
Rich with scent of short-lived
Dainty alpine flowers.
And from the ridgetops I have followed you
Down through heather fields, through timber,
Downward winding to the hoof-churned shore of
One tiny blue-green mountain lake
Untouched by lips of men.

Ancient, wandering trails
Cut and edged by centuries of cloven hooves

Passing from one pasture to another—
Route and destination seeming aimless, but
Charted by the sharp-tempered guardian of creatures,
Instinct. A God coarse-haired, steel-muscled,
Thin-flanked and musky. Used to sleeping lonely
In the snow, or napping in the mountain grasses
On warm summer afternoons, high in the meadows.
And their God laughs low and often
At the man-made trails,
Precise-cut babies of the mountains
Ignorant of the fine, high-soaring ridges
And the slanting grassy meadows
Hanging over space—
Trails that follow streams and valleys
In well-marked switchbacks through the trees,
Newcomers to the Elk world.

(High above, the Elk walk in the evening
From one pasture to another
Scrambling on the rock and snow
While their ancient, wandering,
Aimless trails
And their ancient, coarse-haired,
Thin-flanked God
Laugh in silent wind-like chuckles
At man, and all his trails.)

Mt. St. Helens, Spirit Lake, 1947

LINES ON A CARP

old fat fish of everlasting life
in rank brown pools discarded by the river
soft round-mouth nudging mud
among the reeds, beside the railroad track

you will not hear the human cries
but pines will grow between those ties
before you turn your belly to the sun

A SINECURE FOR P. WHALEN

Whalen, curious vulture,
Picked the Western mind,
Ate the cataracted eyes
That once saw Gwion race the hag
And addle gentlemen

Still unfilled, he skittered to
The sweet bamboo
Fed green on yellow silt
And built a poem to dead Li Po.
The Drunkard taught him how to dance,
Leave dead bodies to the plants,
Sleep out nights in rain.

MESSAGE FROM OUTSIDE

I am the one who gnawed the blanket through
Peeped in the hole and saw with my left eye
The one-leg sliver man put out the fire.

I dug like mice below the cabin's floor
Crawling through oil and rotted hides, I broke
Into that curious handsewn box. Pursued by birds,
Threw my comb, my magic marbles to the wind,
Caught the last bus, and made it here on time.

Stop chewing gum, I show you what I stole—
Pine-marten furs, and box within each box,
The final box in swallow tendons tied,
Inside, an eye! It screws into
The center of your head.

But there they call me urine-boy,
And this deserted newsstand is quite safe.
Peer through this and watch the people spawn:
It makes me laugh, but Raven only croaks.

I saw Coyote! And I'll buy a gun,
Go back and build a monstrous general fire,
Watch the forests move into this town.

You stand cracking sunflower seeds and stare.

UNDER THE SKIN OF IT

Naturally tender, flesh and such
Being entirely mortal, fragile
And complex as a model plane.
Demanding attention, in its unfair ways

Getting, of course, the pleasure that it seeks.

But is it pleased?
Flesh being a type of clay (or dust);
Spirit, the other, like a gas,
Rising and floating in the hollow
Of the Skull—

Which is to know the other's real delight?

Both under the skin, which stretches
As we grow, sagging a trifle
In the pinch of time. Enchanting
The thought of pleasure pleasing flesh and bone.

"DOGS, SHEEP, COWS, GOATS"

dogs, sheep, cows, goats
and sometimes deer, hear loud noises
crackling in bushes, and they flick
fly or creep, as rabbits do
does too, into warm nests. no talk
but chatters there, small throat sounds
ear-pricks, up or back. hooves
tinkle on creekbeds. who fears a talk-
less landscape, crowded with creatures
leaves. falls. undergrowth
crawls all night, and summer smells
deep in the bushes. crouch!
at the thorny stalks.

SEAMAN'S DITTY

I'm wondering where you are now
Married, or mad, or free:
Wherever you are you're likely glad,
But memory troubles me.

We could've had us children,
We could've had a home—
But you thought not, and I thought not,
And these nine years we roam.

Today I worked in the deep dark tanks,
And climbed out to watch the sea:
Gulls and salty waves pass by,
And mountains of Araby.

I've travelled the lonely oceans
And wandered the lonely towns.
I've learned a lot and lost a lot,
And proved the world was round.

Now if we'd stayed together,
There's much we'd never've known—
But dreary books and weary lands
Weigh on me like a stone.

Indian Ocean, 1959

POEM LEFT IN SOURDOUGH MOUNTAIN LOOKOUT

I the poet Gary Snyder
Stayed six weeks in fifty-three
On this ridge and on this rock
& saw what every Lookout sees,
Saw these mountains shift about
& end up on the ocean floor
Saw the wind and waters break
The branched deer, the Eagle's eye,
& when pray tell, shall Lookouts die?

LATE OCTOBER CAMPING IN THE SAWTOOTHS

Sunlight climbs the snowpeak
    glowing pale red
Cold sinks into the gorge
    shadows merge.
Building a fire of pine twigs
    at the foot of a cliff,
Drinking hot tea from a tin cup
    in the chill air—
Pull on sweater and roll a smoke.
    a leaf
    beyond fire
Sparkles with nightfall frost.

POINT REYES

Sandpipers at the margin
        in the moon—
Bright fan of the flat creek
On dark sea sand,
        rock boom beyond:
The work of centuries and wars,
        a car,
Is parked a mile above
        where the dirt road ends.
In naked gritty sand,
Eye-stinging salty driftwood campfire
        smoke, out far,
It all begins again.
Sandpipers chasing the shiny surf
        in the moonlight—
By a fire at the beach.

MAKINGS

I watched my father's friends
Roll cigarettes, when I was young
Leaning against our black tarpaper shack.
The wheatstraw grimy in their hands
Talking of cars and tools and jobs
Everybody out of work.
  the quick flip back
And thin lick stick of the tongue,
And a twist, and a fingernail flare of match.
I watched and wished my overalls
Had hammer-slings like theirs.

The war and after the war
With jobs and money came,
My father lives in a big suburban home.
It seems like since the thirties
I'm the only one stayed poor.
It's good to sit in the
Window of my shack,
Roll tan wheatstraw and tobacco
Round and smoke.

Marin-an

LONGITUDE 170° WEST, LATITUDE 35° NORTH

For Ruth Sasaki

This realm half sky half water,
    night black with white foam
    streaks of glowing fish
    the high half black too lit with
    dots of stars,
The thrum of the diesel engine twirling
    sixty-foot drive shafts of twin screws,
Shape of a boat, and floating
    over a mile of living seawater, underway,
    always westward, dropping
    land behind us to the east,
Brought only these brown Booby birds that trail
    a taste of landfall feathers in the craw
    hatchrock barrens—old migrations—
    flicking from off stern into thoughts,
Sailing jellyfish by day, phosphorescent
    light at night,
    shift of current on the ocean floor
    food chains climbing to the whale.

Ship hanging on this membrane infinitely
    tiny in the "heights" the "deep"
    air-bound beings in the realm of wind
    or water, holding hand to wing or fin
Swimming westward to the farther shore,
    this is what I wanted? so much
    water in the world and so much crossing,
    oceans of truth and seas of doctrine
Salty real seas of our westering world,
    Dharma-spray of lonely slick on deck
Sleepy, between two lands, always a-
    floating world,
            I go below.

                  M. S. Arita Maru, 1956

FOR EXAMPLE

There was an old Dutch lady
Lived in a room in the house
In front of my small shack
Who sat all day in the garden
By my door and read.
She said she knew the East
And once had seen a book
On Buddhist monks. "And you
Gott no business going to
Japan. The thing to be
Is life, is young and travel
Much and love. I know
The way you are, you study hard
But you have friends that
Come and stay, and bike, and
There's the little tree you
Planted by the wall" As I
Filled my water bucket from
A hose. The sun lit up
Her thin white hair a bird
Squawked from the Avocado at the air
& Bodhisattvas teach us everywhere.

BOMB TEST

The fish float belly-up, for real—
Uranium in the whites
            of their eyes
They've been swimming
Deep down where it's black when a
Silvery snow of something queer
                glinted in
From cirrus clouds to the seamounts,
Through all the food chains,
Shrimp to tuna, the currents,
Riding the waves.

Kyoto

DULLNESS IN FEBRUARY: JAPAN

The high-class families
Teach their virgin daughters
English, flowers, and Tea:
Culture of the East—poor girls
Ride boys' bikes balancing noodles.

Brutal sergeants, vicious aesthetes,
     the meeting
Of the worst of East and West.
Silly priests in temples
Far too fine for now.
Discipline for what end?
We gave up wisdom long ago,
Enlightenment is kicks
     —but there is better.
Cold smooth wood floors
And doves, stone pools, moss
Under maples, silent frosty rooftiles
Slanting high—what sense
The old boys made—
Confucius, Lao-tzu, Tu Fu, Sesshu
     and the rest,
Through the centuries, peed off
By politicians in their robes.
Perhaps some flame remains.
     I hope
Again some day
To hit the night road in America
Hitchhiking through dark towns
Rucksack on my back,
To the home of a
Poverty-stricken witty
Drunkard friend.

THE FEATHERED ROBE

For Yaeko Nakamura

On a clear spring windless day
Sea calm, the mountains
    sharp against the sky,
An old man stopped in a sandy
    seashore pine grove,
Lost in the still clear beauty.
Tracing a delicate scent
    he found a splendid robe
Of feathers hanging on a bough.

      Robe over his arm
      He heard   alarm
      Stop, and there he saw
      A shining Lady,
            naked from her swim.

      Without my feathered robe
      that useless-to-you a human,
      Robe, I cannot,
      Home, I
      Cannot fly,
          she cried

And for a dance
    he gave it back.
A dance,
    she wore it glinting in the sun
Pine shadow breeze
Fluttering light sleeves—

      old man watching saw
      all he dreamed in youth

the endless springtime
morning beauty
of the world
    as

She, dancing, rose
Slow floating over pines
High beyond the hills
    a golden speck
In blue sky haze.

          Nō play "Hagoromo"

ON VULTURE PEAK

All the boys are gathered there
Vulture Peak, in the thin air
Watching cycles pass around
From brain to stone and flesh to ground,
Where love and wisdom are the same
But split like light to make the scene,
Ten million camped in a one-room shack
Tracing all the causes back
To Nothing which is not the start
(Now we love, but   here we part)
And not a one can answer why
To the simple garden in my eye.

I.

J.K. & me was squatting naked and sandy
At McClure Beach steaming mussels, eating,
Tossing the shells over our shoulders,
A pair of drunk Siwash starting a shellmound.
Neuri sleeping off a hangover face down
At the foot of a cliff; sea lions off shore

II.

Are bums and drunks truly Angels?
Hairy Immortals drinking poorboys in doorways?
Poor Abelard, thou'rt clipped!
                    the vomit
& prickles of a gritty desert drug
                    sweat and fire
Berry lather & lapping dogs—
                    All babies
Are unborn; tracking the moon through
Flying fenceposts a carload of groceries, home—
What home, pull in park at, and be known?

III.

                    "the little cloud"
A nebula seen slantwise by the naked eye.
The curse of man's humanity to man. "My hair
        is in a pony-tail, I run!"
Each day a lunchpail and a shirtful of sawdust.
Old women dry pods fry corn in the cinders.
The head is a hawk on a boulder
The boulder a nest of coiled snakes

IV.

Nearer than breathing
Closer than skin
                    smack in the earballs
nosehalls, brainpans, tongueclucks
eyeholes, prickbones,
answer! answer! why!
                    "with lowered lids
                    i have entered
                                    nibbana"

V.

Wisdom of the Arab:
            a camel lets her milk down
when tickled in the snatch.
philosophers are horrified
because there is no cause
because everything exists
because the world is real and so are they
and so is nothing is, not nothing save us—
            bony jungle spring
                Shakya in the boondocks.
    a broken start,
            sprout,
        is REALLY gone
                        wow, he

always been standin there
        sweatin' and explainin'?

VI.
    gone where.
Nowhere, where he came from
    thus that thing
    that thus thing
                where were you born from
                born from, born from—
Did you fall   fall   fall
                    fall
    from the salmonberry bough?
Are you the reborn soul
    of a bitter cheated chief?
                    —I came out my mammy
Slick & yapping like a seal
My uncle washed me in the brine
I was a hero & a hunter in my time
A badger gave me visions
A whale made me pure
I sold my wife & children
& jumped into a mirror

VII.
Hot wispy ghosts blown
        down halls between births,
            hobo-jungles of the void—
—Where did we meet last? where
Were you born? Wobblies of the Six
Realms—huddling by some campfire
                    in the stars
Resting & muttering before a birth
On Mars,

VIII.

What can be said about a Rabbit
Solitary and without context
Set before the mind. Was it born?
Has it horns? Dream people walking around
In dream town
          —the city of the Gandharvas—
        not a real city, only the
                        memory of a city—
"The mind dances like the dancer
The intellect's the jester
The senses seem to think the world's a stage—"

IX.

For forty years the Buddha begged his bread
And all those years said nothing, so he said,
& Vulture Peak is silent as a tomb.

STRAITS OF MALACCA 24 OCT 1957

Soft rain on the
gray ocean, a tern
still glides low over
whitecaps
after the ship is gone

Soft rain on
          gray sea
a tern
    glides brushing
               waves
The ship's silent
          wake

Fog of rain on
          water
  Tern glides
  Over waves,
         the
    wake

THE ENGINE ROOM, S.S. SAPPA CREEK

Cool northern waters
Walk around the engine room where
Seven months I worked.

Changing colors
Like seasons in the woods
One week the rails and catwalks all turned red
Valve wheels grow green
Fade with soot and oil,
And bloom again bright yellow after weeks

Paintbrush, pots, & walking round.
The overhead line
Big enough to crawl through
        like I did in Ras Tanura,
Three months ago was white. & now it's
Gray.
Under rusty floorplates
              bilges lap
Venture there in slop of oil & brine
To clean out filters in the fuel oil line.

The engineer said
Paint the hot-lines silver.
I stood on ladders with a silver brush.
Skittering gauges tacked up everywhere
Pressure, pressure on each pump and pipe;
Heat of the steam, heat of the oil,
Heat of the very water where we float
Wrote down in the log book every hour,

Boilers, turbines, nest of bulkheads,
Hatches, doorways, down & sidewise, up,
But no way out.
Sweeping & changing all of it by bits.

—A yard of pipe replaced
A bearing in the trash can.
Me changing less by far—

All that time
Chipping, painting, fixing, this machine.
Lugging wrenches take off manhole covers
Polish tubes, and weld and gasket
            til the damn thing goes,

On land nobody off this ship
Will ever be so free or gay
Though in San Pedro we will
            each man get paid off about
                three thousand dollars cash
In two more days.

THE NORTH COAST

Those picnics covered with sand
No money made them more gay
We passed over hills in the night
And walked along beaches by day.

Sage in the rain, or the sand
Spattered by new-falling rain.
That ocean was too cold to swim
But we did it again and again

ONE YEAR

The hills behind
        Santa Barbara
           from the sea.
Pedro at midnight.
          three thousand dollars
Cash in hundred dollar bills
        —the Wakayama hills—
          each time
A ship hits land the land
       is new.
April. Oakland at eight A.M.
         hotcakes in San Francisco, ten
(Pago a month gone by)
        —jukebox tunes in
           far-off foreign towns;
Mt. Hiei. Tamalpais.
        June. The Desolation
          Valley snow.
She read her poems.
        Sierras in August, always
"Will I ever see those hills again?"
        rain. lightning
         on Whitney
Crackling hair on end.
        Once
         on the coast,
I heard of "Sticky Monkey Flower"
        "It makes you high"
Seals laugh
        in the seaweed—
The mind aches
        seeing a tanker passing
         out at sea.
At Port Townsend on the Sound
        I didn't stop

                    to see Aunt Minnie:
Who gave cookies to my father
                    1910. On Mt. St. Helens
Rotten glaciers turned us back.
                    Hitching home,
                         a German boy from BC
In one sweep drove me down.
                    Columbus Street San Francisco
The bed falls on the floor.
                    months of Marin-an
Learning again the names of birds & trees;
I saw the sea
                    from Santa Barbara,
January. The water always warm.
                    Big Sur in the fog;
In February packed my sleeping bag.
                    Piers, blast
                         whistle & the ship
Backs back & all
                    we never stop to do
                         & think of then
Can cry—lightship, albatross,
                    the ocean like a friend,
Yokohama, Fuji, where its always been—
Mt. Hiei. On the river.
                    settled here.
Today, America, Japan,
                    one year.

THREE POEMS FOR JOANNE

1. LOVING WORDS

Her big basket
        blonde hair drawn back
        over the ears
a directoire, or jacobean feel
        last summer, on crutches
hobbling down the steep hill trail.
sitting beside the geraniums
marking the eucalyptus rustle—sea wind—
                listening
i was chopping wood around the corner
down the hill.
        axe-sound
        the bird
        the wind
    the snorting horses & the starting cars,

loving words—
        "be true
to the *poem*"
nothing will shake that
        fine commitment down.

2. THE HEART OF THE WOOD

The cool
    clearing.
We have never seen
Such trees or
      flowers.
We are bare
In the open.
      here make
      our love

No one will
Watch us.
This place is
  Too far
In.

3. JOANNE MY WIFE

Joanne my wife
why frown
long legs are lovely
        I like yr
        freckld breast
        you butt me at night
                asleep
cry out for mother
hurt wild
like child
in dreams
        I cd write you
    no "love" poem
                so long.

fights and the frown
                at dawn.

CRASH

An old man riding his slow bike
Right down the center of the gravel road
At walking pace to talk to two old women
Bundled firewood balanced on their heads,
Distracted or intense in other mind
I picked the space between him and the two
Without a horn-honk tried to ride
Straight through, he swerved inside,
We soft collided in slow motion,
Motorcycle, man, and bike.
In grooved and rutted gravel powder dirt.
He red-faced cursed me in the local way
As I responded in a fair polite
Level of language, Ohara busses,
Waiting at our rear,
The peasant women waited down the road.
My fault. And he recalled he knew my face
And house, a Yase dweller too,
He said he would be madder,
But knew me now. It was not real
Even while kicking back the crash-bars into line.
Where was my mind.
Hieizan over, and the stream,
And all the cherry trees around
About to bloom—and us not hurt—
He rode away, his old brown overcoat
And rubber work shoes puffing dirt.
I overtook him. Later at the temple
My hands began to tremble:
I saw my inattention,
Tiny moment in the thread,
Was where the whole world could have turned
And gone another way.

Kyoto

SAYING FAREWELL AT THE MONASTERY AFTER HEARING THE OLD MASTER LECTURE ON "RETURN TO THE SOURCE"

At the last turn in the path
        "goodbye—"
        —bending, bowing,
    (moss and a bit of
        wild
            bird–)
down.

Daitoku-ji Monastery

ALABASTER

The leather fringes
 swing on the thighs.
 ah so hot
 only beads to wear are cool

And the girls chests like the mens
 are bare
 in the shade
 but the girls differ though the men are same.

Tanya's bosom like a drawn bow
 Holly like a load of flowers
 Ann's gracious fruits
 Masa brown and slimming down
  from milky dark-veined weight
 and, slighter than the rest,

But strongly dappled in the
 sweltering-shady mind,
 Edie's alabaster breasts.

For the women carpenters of Kitkitdizze

THE YEARS

The years seem to tumble
 faster and faster
 I work harder
 the boys get larger
 planting apple and cherry.

In summer barefoot,
 in winter rubber boots.

Little boys bodies
 soft bellies, tiny nipples,
 dirty hands

New grass coming
 through oakleaf and pine needle
 we'll plant a few more trees
 and watch the night sky turn.

NO SHOES NO SHIRT NO SERVICE

Padding down the street, the
Bushmen, the Paiute, the Cintas Largas
    are refused.
The queens of Crete,
The waiting-ladies of the King of Bundelkhand.
Tārā is kept out,
Bare-breasted on her lotus throne.

    (officially, no one goes through
    unofficially, horses go through,
    carriages go through—)

The barefoot shepherds, the bare-chested warriors

    (what is this gate,
    wide as a highway
    that only mice can enter?)

The cow passed through the window nicely—
Only the tail got stuck,

And the soils of this region will be fertile again
After another round of volcanoes
Nutrient ash—
    Shiva's dancing feet
    (No shoes)

HIGH QUALITY INFORMATION

A life spent seeking it
Like a worm in the earth,
Like a hawk. Catching threads
Sketching bones
Guessing where the road goes.
Lao-tzu says
To forget what you knew is best.
That's what I want:
To get these sights down,
Clear, right to the place
Where they fade
Back into the mind of my times.
The same old circuitry
But some paths color-coded
Empty
And we're free to go.

THE ARTS COUNCIL MEETS IN EUREKA

We held a meeting in Eureka
   far in the corner of the state.
   some flew, but I drove it straight—
   west beside Clear Lake
   through level valleys first,
   then chaparral,
   until we reach the cooler coastal air
   and camped the first night under
   tanbark oak.

Next day saw the tallest tree of all:
clapped our hands and asked for longer life.

Eureka by the bay:
   a nuclear power plant; heaps of chips.
   the sawmills owned by men from far away,
   the heaped up kerf
   of mountainsides of logs.
   stand at the edge of sea air fog,

No one who lives here
   has the power
   to run this town.

ARKTOS

(Pythagoras: She-bears are the hands of Rhea)

Sighing, bursting: steam—sulfur—lava—
Rolling and bubbling up, falls out,
Back in on itself
       curling and licking
          getting hard.

Lichens, oak groves, float in up like cloud shadows
Soft, soft,
Loving plant hands.

Tendrils slip through til they meet
       it pulls taut
Green and quick—sap call swells the hills

       changing cloud mountain
       changing cloud gate

Rainbow glimmering with swallows, looping cranes.

       icefields and snowfields ring
       as she comes
       gliding down the rainbow bridge

       Joy of the Mountains
       "The Great She Bear"

FEAR NOT

Will Dallas grow, or wither?
  said the paper.
"Let the bastards freeze in the dark."

    dead or alive?
    knocking at the stone door.
"Goat ropers need love too."
    embracing more than "being"
    the stone door knocks back.

Two women masturbate a corpse,
                        in clay,
One holds his chin—

The Fox-girls switch from
    human to fox-form
    right during the party!
        one man
who was doing cunnilingus on his friend,
    now finds a mouth
    of fur.
The saké bottles clatter down.
    and daylight; all's well,
    just a little sore—

Who's there?
No one who

WE MAKE OUR VOWS
TOGETHER WITH ALL BEINGS

Eating a sandwich
At work in the woods,

As a doe nibbles buckbrush in snow
Watching each other,
chewing together.

A Bomber from Beale
over the clouds,
Fills the sky with a roar.

She lifts head, listens,
Waits till the sound has gone by.

So do I.

AT WHITE RIVER ROADHOUSE
IN THE YUKON

For Gary Holthaus

At White River Roadhouse in the Yukon
A bell rings in the late night:
A lone car on the Alaska highway
Hoping to buy gas at the shut roadhouse.

For a traveller sleeping in a little room
The bell ring is a temple in Japan,
In dream I put on robes and sandals
Chant sūtras in the chilly Buddha-hall.

Ten thousand miles of White Spruce taiga.
The roadhouse master wakes to the night bell
Enters the dark of ice and stars,
To sell the car some gas.

THE PERSIMMONS

In a cove reaching back between ridges
the persimmon groves:
leaves rust-red in October
ochre and bronze
scattering down from the
hard slender limbs of this
slow-growing hardwood
that takes so much nitrogen
and seven years to bear,
and plenty of water all summer
to be bearing so much and so well
as these groves are this autumn.
Gathered in yard-wide baskets
of loose open weave
with mounds of persimmons just picked
still piled on the ground.
On tricycle trucks
pedaled so easy and slow down the lanes,
"Deep tawnie cullour" of sunset
each orb some light left from summer
glowing on brown fall ground,
the persimmons are flowing
on streams of more bike-trucks
til they riffle and back up
alongside a car road
and are spread on the gravel by sellers.
The kind with a crease round the middle,
Tamopan, sweet when soft,
ripening down from the top to the base.
Persimmons and farmers
a long busy line on the roadside,
in season, a bargain, a harvest
of years, the peace of
this autumn again, familiar,
when found by surprise at

the tombs of the dead Ming emperors.
Acres of persimmon orchards
surrounding the tumuli
of kings who saw to it they kept on consuming
even when empty and gone.
The persimmons outlive them,
but up on the hills
where the Great Wall wanders
the oaks had been cut for lumber or charcoal
by Genghis Khan's time.
People and persimmon orchards prevail.
I walked the Great Wall today,
and went deep in the dark of a tomb.
And then found a persimmon
ripe to the bottom
one of a group on a rough plaited tray
that might have been drawn by Mu Ch'i,
tapping its infant-soft skin
to be sure that it's ready,
the old man laughing,
he sees that I like my persimmons.
I trade him some coin
for this wealth of fall fruit
lined up on the roadside to sell to the tourists
who have come to see tombs,
and are offered as well
the people and trees that prevail.

Beijing, People's Republic, 1984

Tiny
Energies

For such situations of a few combinations found in messages, the energy content as a fuel is far too negligible to measure or consider compared to the great flows of energy in the food chain. Yet the quality of this energy (tiny energies in the right form) is so high that in the right control circuit it may obtain huge amplifications and control vast flows of power.

—H.T. Odum, *Environment Power and Society*

THROUGH

The white spot of a Flicker
    receding through cedar

Fluttering red surveyors tapes
    through trees, the dark woods

❧

FOR BERKELEY

City of buds and flowers

Where are your fruits?

Where are your
    roots.

❧

WHAT HISTORY FAILS TO MENTION IS

Most everybody lived their lives
With friends and children, played it cool,
Left truth & beauty to the guys
Who tricked for bigshots, and were fools.

❧

HOME ON THE RANGE

Bison rumble-belly
Bison shag coat
Bison sniffing bison body
Bison skull looking at the sweat lodge.
Bison liver warm. Bison flea
Bison paunch stew.
Bison baby falls down.
Bison skin home. Bison bedding,
"Home on the Range."

❧

THE OTHER SIDE OF EACH COIN

The head of a man of the ruling elite
And a very large building.
One on each side of the coin

❧

SERVES

A human arm
bone is the best
bone for a
bone chisel.
A corn cob
serves as a cork.

(As stated by: Captain Cook, and an elder lady of Zuni.)

❧

Lots of play

in the way things work,
in the way things are.

History is made of mistakes.

yet—on the surface—
the world looks OK

lots of play.

♨

KNOW

The trees know
stars to be sources

Like the sun,
of their life;

But many   and tiny
sprinkled through the dark

When,
where has the sun gone—

♨

There are those who love to get dirty
    and fix things.
They drink coffee at dawn,
    beer after work,

And those who stay clean,
    just appreciate things,
At breakfast they have milk
    and juice at night.

There are those who do both,
    they drink tea.

※

LIZARDS, WIND, SUNSHINE, APPLES

a plane circling in the distance
a football game on the radio in the barn
an axe chopping in the woods
a chicken pecking catfood in the kitchen.

※

HOW ZEN MASTERS ARE LIKE MATURE HERRING

So few become full grown
And how necessary all the others;
    gifts to the food chain,
    feeding another universe.

These big ones feed sharks.

No
Nature

HOW POETRY COMES TO ME

It comes blundering over the
Boulders at night, it stays
Frightened outside the
Range of my campfire
I go to meet it at the
Edge of the light

ON CLIMBING THE SIERRA MATTERHORN AGAIN AFTER THIRTY-ONE YEARS

Range after range of mountains
Year after year after year.
I am still in love.

4 X 40086, On the summit

KUŠIWOQQÓBɨ

Did it come from
The ice age lakes and streams?
Flows of liquid rock
The salt of seas,
Wind on hills for years,
This day's sun and trees?
Or this one nose?
The smell in the bark of
                Jeffrey Pine.

My nose poked in the bark
Went a million years—
Sweet smell of the pine.

Delicious! Like pineapple!
What did the Piute children think of,
Smelling *Kušiwoqqóbɨ,*
What did they say?

Sun glittering on obsidian,
Wind on a hundred peaks,
Hugging a tree, smelling the bark,
I thought I heard "Kušiwoqqóbɨ"
A soft voice from across,

From the dust, from the breeze.

VII 82, Trip with Kai down the east side
near Mammoth

THE SWEAT

For John and Jan Straley

Now I must sit naked.

Socks and glasses tucked into my moccasins,
Wearing only earrings and a faded tattoo—

On a cedar bench too hot to touch,
Buttocks take it—legs fold,
Back eases on to the burning wall
Sweating and the in-breath cooled
Through a wet-soaked towel
—old Aleut trick—
And look out the small window
On a snow-capped volcano
And inside toward the stove, the
Women who sweat here
And groan and laugh with the heat,

The women speak of birth at home.
Of their children, their breasts hang
Softer, the nipples darker,
Eyes clear and warm.
Naked. Legs up, we have all raised children,

I could love each one,
Their ease, their opened—sweet—
    older—still youthful—
    womanly being bodies—

And outside, naked, cooling on the deck
Midsummer's far northern soft dusk eve,
Bare skin to the wind;

Older is smarter and more tasty.
Minds tough and funny—many lovers—
At the end of days of talking
Science, writing, values, spirit, politics, poems—

Different shoes and shirts,
In little heaps—sit naked, silent, gaze
On chests and breasts and knees and knobby feet
   in the tide smell, on the bleached deck planks,
Like seals hauled out for sunning,

Crinkles by the eyes,
Limber legs crossed,
Single mothers—past parenting—
Back to college—running a business—
Checking salmon for the Fish & Game,
Writing a play, an article, a novel,
Waitressing and teaching,
In between men friends, teen-age son—
Doing a dissertation on the Humpbacked Whales,
Doing tough-assed poems—

Naked comfort, scant fear,
Strong soul, naught to hide,

This life:
We get old enough and finally really like it!
Meeting and sweating
At a breezy beach.

VI 87, Baranoff Island, Alaska

BUILDING

We started our house midway through the Cultural Revolution,
The Vietnam war, Cambodia, in our ears,
    tear gas in Berkeley,
Boys in overalls with frightened eyes, long matted hair, ran
    from the police.
We peeled trees, drilled boulders, dug sumps, took sweat baths
    together.
That house finished we went on
Built a schoolhouse, with a hundred wheelbarrows,
    held seminars on California paleo-indians during lunch.
We brazed the Chou dynasty form of the character "Mu"
    on the blacksmithed brackets of the ceiling of the lodge,
Buried a five-prong vajra between the schoolbuildings
    while praying and offering tobacco.
Those buildings were destroyed by a fire, a pale copy rebuilt
    by insurance.

Ten years later we gathered at the edge of a meadow.
The cultural revolution is over, hair is short,
    the industry calls the shots in the Peoples Forests,
Single mothers go back to college to become lawyers.

Blowing the conch, shaking the staff-rings
    we opened work on a Hall.
Forty people, women carpenters, child labor, pounding nails,
Screw down the corten roofing and shape the beams
    with a planer,
The building is done in three weeks.
We fill it with flowers and friends and open it up.

Now in the year of the Persian Gulf,
Of Lies and Crimes in the Government held up as Virtues,
    this dance with Matter
Goes on: our buildings are solid, to live, to teach, to sit,
To sit, to know for sure the sound of a bell—

This is history. This is outside of history.
Buildings are built in the moment,
    they are constantly wet from the pool
        that renews all things
    naked and gleaming.

The moon moves
Through her twenty-eight nights.
Wet years and dry years pass;
Sharp tools, good design.

SURROUNDED BY WILD TURKEYS

Little calls   as they pass
   through dry forbs and grasses
Under blue oak and gray digger pine
In the warm afternoon of the forest-fire haze;

Twenty or more, long-legged birds
   all alike.

So are we, in our soft calling,
   passing on through.

Our young, which trail after,

Look just like us.

OFF THE TRAIL

for Carole

We are free to find our own way
Over rocks—through the trees—
Where there are no trails. The ridge and the forest
Present themselves to our eyes and feet
Which decide for themselves
In their old learned wisdom of doing
Where the wild will take us. We have
Been here before. It's more intimate somehow
Than walking the paths that lay out some route
That you stick to,
All paths are possible, many will work,
Being blocked is its own kind of pleasure,
Getting through is a joy, the side-trips
And detours show down logs and flowers,
The deer paths straight up, the squirrel tracks
Across, the outcroppings lead us on over.
Resting on treetrunks,
Stepping out on the bedrock, angling and eyeing
Both making choices—now parting our ways—
And later rejoin; I'm right, you're right,
We come out together. *Mattake,* "Pine Mushroom,"
Heaves at the base of a stump. The dense matted floor
Of Red Fir needles and twigs. This is wild!
We laugh, wild for sure,
Because no place is more than another,
All places total,
And our ankles, knees, shoulders &
Haunches know right where they are.
Recall how the *Dao De*
Jing puts it: the trail's not the way.
No path will get you there, we're off the trail,

You and I, and we chose it! Our trips out of doors
Through the years have been practice
For this ramble together,
Deep in the mountains
Side by side,
Over rocks, through the trees.

WORD BASKET WOMAN

Years after surviving
the Warsaw uprising,
she wrote the poems of ordinary people
building barricades while being shot at,
small poems were all
that could hold so much
close to death   life
without making it false.

Robinson Jeffers, his tall cold view
quite true in a way, but why did he say it
as though he alone
stood above our delusions, he also
feared death, insignificance,
and was not quite up to the inhuman beauty
of parsnips or diapers, the deathless
nobility   at the core of all ordinary things

I dwell
in a house on the long west slope
of Sierra Nevada, two hundred mile
swell of granite,
bones of the Ancient Buddha,
miles back from the seacoast
on a line of fiery chakras
in the deep nerve web of the land,

Europe forgotten now, almost a dream—
but our writing
is sidewise and roman, and the language
a compote of old wars and tribes from some
place overseas. Here
at the rim of the world
where the *panaka* calls in the *chá*—the heart
words are Pomo, Miwok, Nisenan,

and the small poem word baskets
stretch to the heft of their burden.

I came this far to tell
of the grave of my great-
grandmother Harriet Callicotte
by itself on a low ridge in Kansas.
The sandstone tumbled,
her name almost eaten away,
where I found it in rain drenched grass
on my knees, closed my eyes
and swooped under the earth
to that loam dark, holding her emptiness
and placed one cool kiss
on the arch of her white
pubic bone.

VI 85, Carneiro Kansas
XII 87, Kitkitdizze

AT TOWER PEAK

Every tan rolling meadow will turn into housing
Freeways are clogged all day
Academies packed with scholars writing papers
City people lean and dark
This land most real
As its western-tending golden slopes
And bird-entangled central valley swamps
Sea-lion, urchin coasts
Southerly salmon-probes
Into the aromatic almost-Mexican hills
Along a range of granite peaks
The names forgotten,
An eastward running river that ends out in desert
The chipping ground-squirrels in the tumbled blocks
The gloss of glacier ghost on slab
Where we wake refreshed from ten hours sleep
After a long day's walking
Packing burdens to the snow
Wake to the same old world of no names,
No things, new as ever, rock and water,
Cool dawn birdcalls, high jet contrails.
A day or two or million, breathing
A few steps back from what goes down
In the current realm.
A kind of ice age, spreading, filling valleys
Shaving soils, paving fields, you can walk it
Live in it, drive through it   then
It melts away
For whatever sprouts
After the age of
Frozen hearts. Flesh-curved rock
And gusts on the summit,
Smoke from forest fires is white,
The haze above the distant valley like a dusk.

It's just one world, this spine of rock and streams
And snow, and the wash of gravels, silts
Sands, bunchgrasses, saltbrush, bee-fields,
Twenty million human people, downstream, here below.

RIGHT IN THE TRAIL

Here it is, near the house,
A **big** pile, fat scats,
Studded with those deep red
Smooth-skinned manzanita berries,
Such a pile! Such droppings,
Awesome. And I saw how
The young girl in the story,
Had good cause to comment
On the bearscats she found while
Picking blueberries with her friends.
She laughed at them
Or maybe **with** them, jumped over them
(Bad luck!), and is reported
To have said "wide anus!"
To amuse or annoy the Big Brown Ones
Who are listening, of course.

They say the ladies
Have always gone berrying
And they all join together
To go out for the herring spawn,
Or to clean green salmon.
And that big set of lessons
On what bears really want,
Was brought back by the girl
Who made those comments:
She was taken on a year-long excursion
Deep in the mountains,
Through the tangled deadfalls,
Down into the den.
She had some pretty children by a
Young and handsome Bear.

Now I'm on the dirt
Looking at these scats

And I want to cry not knowing why
At the honor and the humor
Of coming on this sign
That is not found in books
Or transmitted in letters,
And is for women just as much as men,
A shining message for all species,
A glimpse at the Trace
Of the Great One's passing,
With a peek into her whole wild system—
And what was going on last week,
(Mostly still manzanita)—

Dear Bear: do stay around. Be good.
And though I know
It won't help to say this,

Chew your food.

TRAVELLING TO THE CAPITAL

I put on my travelling clothes
          and went up to the Capital
          to see the blooming cherries—

Elderly sakura blossoming
          east of the huge library
          loosing petals to the winds.

We walked by miles of buildings
          past sheets of clear pool water
          men begging on the street
          where people come to eat

We stand in the grass in the open—
          hear jet plane takeoff rumble
          fill the whole downtown.
          go read poems with friends
          in a theater made for Shakespeare,
          have a party with the crowd—

An elderly black man caterer
          pours drinks at a table,
          I ask him why the channel-locks?
          he says "For the Perrier"

This our little nation,
          —our capital, its blossoms—
          its library for the people
          our nation of bison and grass. Those
          days of woods and glades,

Those days are gone.
                              we get,
This dolphin-drowned,
This waste-tormented sea.

                    Spring 89, Washington

THOUGHTS ON LOOKING AT A SAMUEL PALMER
ETCHING AT THE TATE

Moonlight landscape, sheep,
     and shepherds watching eerie beauty

The broad sheep backs
     resting bunched up under leafy oaks
     or hid in black moon shadow,

Lives of cows and sheep—
     calf mouth that sucks your finger
     the steer that pokes his head through
     pipe iron gate
     to lick lapel, and lightly
     touch and taste
     the buttons of your coat,

Cows that trail you as you cross the meadow;
     & silent sheep   slow heads turning
     solemn faces
     hooves fringed in dewy grass.

They stamp and steam in chilly morn
     and gaze at length on clouds and hills

       before they board the truck.

82, Devon & London

KISIABATON

Beat-up datsun idling in the road
shreds of fog
almost-vertical hillsides drop away
huge stumps fading into mist
soft warm rain

Snaggy, forked and spreading tops, a temperate cloud-forest tree

Chamaecyparis formosiana—
    Taiwan hinoki,
        hung-kuai   red cypress

That the tribal people call   *kisiabaton*

this rare old tree
is what we came to see.

IX 90, Ali-shan, Taiwan

FOR LEW WELCH IN A SNOWFALL

Snowfall in March:
I sit in the white glow reading a thesis
About you. Your poems, your life.

The author's my student,
He even quotes me.

Forty years since we joked in a kitchen in Portland
Twenty since you disappeared.

All those years and their moments—
Crackling bacon, slamming car doors,
Poems tried out on friends,
Will be one more archive,
One more shaky text.

But life continues in the kitchen
Where we still laugh and cook,
Watching snow.

III 91, Kitkitdizze

RIPPLES ON THE SURFACE

"Ripples on the surface of the water—
were silver salmon passing under—different
from the ripples caused by breezes"

A scudding plume on the wave—
a humpback whale is
breaking out in air up
gulping herring
          —Nature not a book, but a *performance,* a
high old culture

Ever-fresh events
scraped out, rubbed out, and used, used, again—
the braided channels of the rivers
hidden under fields of grass—

The vast wild
          the house, alone.
The little house in the wild,
          the wild in the house.
Both forgotten.

                    No nature

          Both together, one big empty house.

INDEX